Trapped

WHEN ACTING ETHICALLY IS AGAINST THE LAW

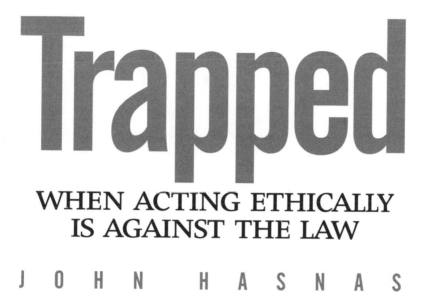

Trapped

WHEN ACTING ETHICALLY IS AGAINST THE LAW

JOHN HASNAS

CATO INSTITUTE
WASHINGTON, D.C.

Library of Congress Cataloging-in-Publication Data

Hasnas, John.
  Trapped : when acting ethically is against the law / John Hasnas.
    p. cm.
  Includes bibliographical references.
  ISBN 1-930865-88-0 (alk. paper)   1. White collar crimes—United States.   I. Title.

HV6769.H37 2006
364.16'80973—dc22   2006040541

Cover design by Jon Meyers.
Printed in the United States of America.

CATO INSTITUTE
1000 Massachusetts Ave., N.W.
Washington, D.C. 20001
www.cato.org

*For Irving and Doris who made me, and
Ann and Annette who sustain me.*

Contents

1. Introduction

Before reading this book, please take the following multiple-choice quiz:

1. You are the chief executive officer (CEO) of Marsha Tudor Styles Inc., one of the country's largest retailers of products for homemakers. MTS is highly profitable and is closely identified with its founder and chair of the board of directors, Marsha Tudor, who also publishes a magazine and hosts a television show about homemaking. Recently, the Securities and Exchange Commission investigated Tudor for suspected insider trading for selling $1 million of stock in a company owned by a personal friend, just before a sharp decline in the price of that stock. In the course of her voluntary cooperation with the investigation, Tudor stated that she sold the stock pursuant to a pre-established stop-loss order. When news of the investigation became public, Tudor asserted her innocence of insider trading on a national news program. Although Tudor has not been charged with insider trading, she has been indicted for obstruction of justice for telling federal investigators that she sold her stock pursuant to a stop-loss order, as well as for securities fraud for attempting to prop up the value of MTS stock by falsely proclaiming her innocence to the public. You have known Tudor for many years and tend to believe that she is innocent of the charges, although you cannot be entirely sure. In this situation, which of the following constitutes the ethically appropriate action for you to take in your capacity as CEO?

   a. Publicly support Tudor and offer whatever aid the corporation can give her in her effort to clear her name.
   b. Take no action. This matter does not concern the corporation.
   c. Consult with corporate counsel and immediately take steps designed to protect the corporation against any potential civil

1

liability and to preserve its defenses against any potential criminal charges.

    d. Ask Tudor to resign as chair of the board of directors until her legal troubles are resolved and cooperate with the government's criminal investigation of Tudor to the extent that doing so is consistent with preserving the company's legal defenses and respecting all promises of confidentiality, including those granted by corporate counsel under the attorney-client privilege.

    e. Authorize the corporation to plead guilty to securities fraud and aid the government's criminal investigation of Tudor in every way, including waiving the corporation's attorney-client privilege and turning over records of all Tudor's appointments, phone calls, e-mails, and confidential consultations with the corporate counsel.

2. You are a senior executive at the Stone Fund, a large mutual fund company. The majority of investors in the Stone Fund are small investors, but the fund has several large investors as well as several institutional investors. Until recently, Gordon Gekko was one of the fund's most successful manager-brokers. He was responsible for acquiring most of the large investors in the fund. He apparently did this by allowing several of these investors to make trades after 4:00 p.m., which is illegal. Budd Fox, a junior broker who worked for Gekko, processed many of the late trades. Fox, who had been hired right out of business school, was not aware at first that he was doing anything wrong. Gekko's high status in the company, his forceful personality, and his assurance that the late trades were perfectly acceptable and were standard operating procedure in the industry led Fox to carry out Gekko's orders without qualm. Eventually becoming suspicious, Fox approached Stone Fund's corporate counsel in confidence to inquire about the legality of his actions. On learning of the late trades, Stone Fund immediately fired Gekko and reported his actions to the Department of Justice and the Securities and Exchange Commission. Which of the following constitutes the ethically appropriate action for you to take with respect to Fox?

    a. Assign him to work with a broker who can serve as an ethical mentor, and use the legal resources of the company to help him defend himself against any criminal charges that may be brought as a result of his association with Gekko.

b. Allow him to continue working for the company, but do not use corporate resources to aid him in defending any criminal charges that are brought against him personally.

c. Fire him.

d. Fire him and recommend that the company report his activities to the Department of Justice and Securities and Exchange Commission.

e. Fire him and recommend that the company not only report his activities to the DOJ and the SEC but also offer to cooperate with the prosecutors in building a case against him by waiving the company's attorney-client privilege and turning over to the government any evidence that could possibly aid in establishing his guilt.

3. You are the new CEO of Endrun Inc., a very troubled corporation. Acting without the knowledge of Endrun's former CEO, Kevin Lie, the company's chief operating officer (COO) and chief accounting officer (CAO) had been using improper accounting practices to disguise the size of the company's debt and inflate the company's profits. When this fraud came to light, Endrun was forced to restate its earnings for the past several years, causing the company to suffer serious losses in the third and fourth quarters as well as a sharp decline in the price of its stock. The COO and CAO have since pled guilty to securities and wire fraud, and Lie resigned as CEO. You stepped in to try to staunch the bleeding and revive the company. You have just learned that Lie has been indicted for wire fraud for statements he made at an "All Employee Meeting" video teleconference. At that meeting, Lie said:

- "The third quarter is looking great. We will hit our numbers. We are continuing to have strong growth in our businesses, and I think we are positioned for a strong fourth quarter."

- "I have strongly encouraged our officers to buy additional Endrun stock. Some, including myself, have done so over the past couple of months, and others will probably do so in the future. My personal belief is that Endrun stock is an incredible bargain at current prices."

3

- "Liquidity is fine. As a matter of fact, it's better than fine—it's strong."

The indictment claims that these statements constitute a scheme and artifice to defraud Endrun and its shareholders of their intangible right to Lie's honest services because:

- With regard to the first statement, Lie knew that Endrun was about to announce a quarterly loss for the third quarter and was aware that lowering the previous earning statements was going to adversely affect the company.
- With regard to the second statement, Lie deliberately created the impression among Endrun employees that his confidence in the company's stock was such that he had increased his personal ownership of Endrun stock in the "past couple of months," when, in fact, he had purchased approximately $4 million in Endrun stock but sold $24 million in Endrun stock in response to margin calls during that period. The sales were concealed from Endrun employees and the rest of the investing public.
- With regard to the third statement, Lie knew that the only readily available source of liquidity was the $3 billion corporate line of credit, which, if drawn, would signal the dire straits of Endrun's finances.

Lie claims that none of his statements were false, that at the time he made them he genuinely believed Endrun could overcome its problems, that he was acting responsibly as CEO to maintain employee morale in a time of crisis, and that the charges against him are driven by political pressure to find a scapegoat for employee and investor losses on the stock market. Which of the following constitutes the ethically appropriate action for you to take as CEO?

a. Publicly support Lie, offer whatever aid the corporation can give him in defending himself against the charges, and honor the company's policy of reimbursing the legal expenses of corporate officers who incur such expenses as a result of their activities on behalf of the corporation.
b. Honor the company's legal expense reimbursement policy, but take no other action with regard to Lie's case.

c. Honor the company's legal expense reimbursement policy, consult with corporate counsel to determine the extent to which Lie's situation creates the risk of civil or criminal liability for the corporation, and take appropriate steps to defend against such liability.

d. Honor the company's legal expense reimbursement policy but cooperate with the government's criminal investigation of Mr. Lie to the extent that doing so is consistent with preserving the company's legal defenses and respecting all promises of confidentiality, including those granted by corporate counsel under the attorney-client privilege.

e. Do not honor the company's legal expense reimbursement policy for Lie, authorize the corporation to plead guilty to wire fraud, and aid the government's criminal investigation of Lie in every way, including waiving the corporation's attorney-client privilege, turning over all corporate documents that may bear on the case, and attempting to recover and turn over any corporate documents that Lie may have in his personal possession.

Thank you for taking the quiz. The purpose of this book is to explore how federal efforts to combat white-collar crime bear on the answers to these and similar questions.

Specifically, I intend to examine how the federal standard for corporate criminal responsibility, the requirements of several of the federal statutes used to combat white-collar crime, and the incentives created by the U.S. Sentencing Commission's Federal Sentencing Guidelines for Organizations[1] influence the decisions of businesspeople confronted with difficult ethical dilemmas. I will suggest that, in the context of federal criminal law, there are many ways in which compliance is not ethical and ethical behavior is not compliance. As a result, the current federal campaign against white-collar crime frequently undermines, rather than enhances, the efforts of businesspeople to behave ethically.

The predominate response to the recent corporate scandals within the business community has been to call for renewed efforts to ensure that businesspeople behave more ethically and obey the law. This response reflects two assumptions that businesspeople often accept uncritically: that the law commands only ethical behavior and that businesspeople who behave ethically have nothing to fear from the law. Although those assumptions may generally be true, they patently are not true in an increasing number of cases that can produce achingly poignant situations for businesspeople who act in naive reliance on them.

The sole professional obligation of federal prosecutors is to punish and, to whatever extent possible, prevent violation of federal criminal law. In most cases, businesspeople, too, have an obligation to ensure that members of their firms do not violate federal law, but this obligation is not their only, or even their primary, one. In current business terminology, businesspeople have obligations to their stakeholders. They have a fiduciary duty to their principals, the stockholders, to use the stockholders' resources only as authorized and to advance the purposes for which the firm was organized. They have contractual, as well as informal customary, obligations to their employees, customers, and suppliers. Furthermore, they have their ordinary ethical obligations as human beings to honor their commitments and to deal honestly with others. Those obligations can, and to an increasing extent do, conflict with the obligation to take the most effective steps to comply with federal law. When the law provides incentives to violate one's ethical duties to others, businesspeople face a difficult choice. Federal prosecutors do not. Businesspeople must decide the extent to which they can ethically expose their firm to the risk of legal liability in order to meet their other obligations. Federal prosecutors, whose only obligation is to the law, need only judge the level of the firm's legal compliance. Simply expressed, businesspeople's ethical dilemmas are not the federal prosecutors' problem.

In this book, I intend to explore the ethical difficulties this divergence of interests poses for those engaged in business. In Part I, I will introduce what is perhaps an idiosyncratic definition of "white-collar crime" to distinguish the efforts of the federal government to combat business-related crime from traditional state-level criminal enforcement. I will then identify the special difficulties that the traditional rules of criminal law pose for federal efforts to police business activity and will detail the substantive and procedural innovations that were introduced into federal criminal law to surmount these difficulties. In Part II, I will identify five areas in which these legal innovations create difficult ethical dilemmas for the conscientious businessperson. Specifically, I will argue that these innovations make it more difficult for businesses to realize organizational justice, to properly respect employees' privacy, to maintain needed confidentiality, to engender trust within the organization, and to engage in ethical self-assessment. Finally, I will provide an explanation for the divergence between ethics and compliance and will suggest that the solution to the problem of white-collar crime may not lie in using harsher measures to crack down on white-collar criminals, but in restraining the power of federal prosecutors to do so at all.

PART I

THE EVOLUTION OF WHITE-COLLAR CRIME

2. The Nature of White-Collar Crime

White-collar crime can be defined in many ways. It has been defined as crime committed by a person of respectable or high social status[1] or in the course of one's occupation,[2] as crime that involves deceit or a breach of trust,[3] as nonviolent crime undertaken for personal gain,[4] as crime that involves a combination of these factors,[5] and simply as business crime.[6] None of these definitions specifies the class of offenses that I wish to address in this book, however. I intend to restrict my focus to federal law, and then even more narrowly to the particular subset of federal law that is designed to police the behavior of those engaged in business for honest dealing and compliance with regulatory requirements. Because all of the above definitions include state offenses, and many include nonbusiness-related crime as well, none of them correspond to the class of offense that I am interested in. Accordingly, for purposes of this book, I will employ the phrase "white-collar crime" in a somewhat idiosyncratic manner to refer exclusively to behavior that is the object of federal efforts to ensure honest dealing and regulatory compliance in business.

Under this stipulative definition, white-collar criminal law constitutes a discrete subset of American criminal law. It is distinct from state criminal law, which is directed against actions that either directly harm or violate the rights of others or constitute what is regarded as inherently immoral activity—the so-called morals offenses or victimless crimes. This traditional understanding of crime, which is the subject of the typical first-year law school course in criminal law, covers offenses such as murder, rape, kidnapping, and theft, as well as prostitution, the use of illegal narcotics, and, somewhat famously, taking a girl under the age of 16 out of the care of her parents without their consent. White-collar crime is also distinct from much of federal criminal law, which, in addition to prohibiting offenses of purely national concern such as treason or counterfeiting, prohibits "traditional" criminal activity when that activity transcends state boundaries. As used in this book, the term white-collar crime refers exclusively to the class of federal offenses designed to police business behavior that do not fit within those categories.

The distinction between ordinary and white-collar criminal law is perhaps best illustrated by a comparison of what constitutes fraudulent behavior under each. State law criminalizes fraudulent conduct when it amounts to larceny by false pretenses.[7] To establish the offense of false pretenses, "the prosecutor was required to prove that [the] defendant obtained title or possession of money or personal property of another by means of an intentional false statement concerning a material fact upon which the victim relied in parting with the property."[8] False pretenses criminalizes dishonest behavior only when it is intended to obtain and is effective in obtaining property on the basis of a representation of fact that is known to be false and that the other party actually relies upon.[9] This interpretation depends on a fairly strict set of requirements that punishes dishonesty only when it causes significant harm to others.

The epitome of white-collar criminal law is the federal mail fraud statute.[10] To establish the offense of mail fraud, the prosecution must show only that the defendant intentionally participated in a scheme or artifice to defraud that involves use of the mail or a private carrier service.[11] This statute criminalizes dishonest behavior intended to deprive others of property or of the intangible right to another person's honest services[12] on the basis of a false representation or promise, regardless of whether anyone actually relies on the representation or promise or is deprived of property or honest services.[13] These broad provisions authorize the punishment of almost any kind of dishonest or deceptive behavior, even when no other party has suffered any harm. Thus, mail fraud charges have been brought against a developer for attempting to sell homes by falsely claiming that they were good investments[14] and against a physician for referring patients to a hospital without disclosing to the patients that the hospital paid him a fee for the referrals.[15]

The mail fraud statute is typical of white-collar crime in that it empowers the federal government to police dishonest conduct that is otherwise beyond the scope of traditional criminal law. Other offenses that share this feature and thus fall within the white-collar crime category are general offenses such as wire, bank, and securities fraud, as well as violations of the Racketeer Influenced and Corrupt Organizations Act, specific offenses that involve a violation of federal

12

regulations, and subsidiary offenses such as money laundering, making false statements to federal investigators, and obstruction of justice. For purposes of this book, those offenses constitute the realm of white-collar crime.

3. Problems of Enforcement

Both the substantive and procedural rules of traditional Anglo-American criminal law have evolved over the course of centuries in the crucible of the conflict between Parliament and the Crown for power and the struggle to preserve the "rights of Englishmen" against the prerogatives of the king. This is not the place to retell this tale other than to observe that by the beginning of the 20th century, the process had produced a body of criminal law that contained many civil libertarian features. Three such features that resided within the substantive criminal law were the *mens rea* requirement, the absence of vicarious criminal liability, and the principle of legality.

The *mens rea* requirement limited the state to punishing those individuals who acted with a "guilty" mind—that is, those who intentionally or recklessly engaged in prohibited conduct or produced a prohibited consequence.[1] This limitation provided significant protection for individual liberty in two ways. First, although "[a]cts can occur accidentally . . . the state of mind that accompanies one's act is entirely within the individual's control. Thus, by recognizing *mens rea* as an indispensable element of crimes, we substantially increase the individual's power to control his freedom from punishment."[2] Second, the burden of establishing what was in a defendant's mind is often a significant hurdle for the prosecution to overcome.[3]

Additional protection for individual liberty arose from permitting punishment only for an individual's own actions.[4] In the words of a contemporary commentator, vicarious criminal liability, "by departing from the ordinary principles of causation and from the fundamental, intensely personal, basis of criminal liability, violates the most deep-rooted traditions of criminal law. Vicarious liability is a conception repugnant to every instinct of the criminal jurist."[5] As a result, "[w]hile the civil courts were . . . evolving [*respondeat superior*] during the eighteenth and nineteenth centuries . . . in the law of torts, no such development took place in the criminal law."[6]

15

Another significant substantive protection for liberty was embodied in the principle of legality. Frequently encapsulated in the Latin phrase *nullum crimen sine lege, nulla poena sine lege* (no crime or punishment without law), the principle of legality holds that "conduct is not criminal unless forbidden by law which gives advance warning that such conduct is criminal."[7] The principle is operationalized in the form of four corollaries: (1) a ban on retroactive criminal lawmaking; (2) a ban on the judicial creation of new common law crimes; (3) a requirement that criminal offenses be clearly enough defined to give citizens adequate notice of what conduct is prohibited and to establish clear guidelines governing law enforcement; and (4) a requirement that the language of a criminal offense be strictly construed in favor of the defendant (the rule of lenity).[8] All four corollaries "are reflective of the central values of liberal societies"[9] in that they serve to ensure that "people are entitled to know what they are forbidden to do so that they may shape their conduct accordingly . . . [and] to eliminate the oppressive and arbitrary exercise of official discretion."[10] The latter two corollaries, which are the ones of concern in the present context, place significant limits on both the breadth of the criminal statutes that the legislature may enact and the range of application of those that are duly enacted.

Many procedural protections for liberty also evolved. The most famous of these are the twin requirements that the accused must be presumed to be innocent until proven guilty and that the state must establish the accused's guilt beyond reasonable doubt. The presumption of innocence means that the innocence of the defendant is assumed and that the state bears the burden of introducing evidence sufficient to establish every element of a criminal offense.[11] The requirement of proof beyond reasonable doubt sets the bar that the state must surmount to establish those elements exceedingly high. Taken together, these requirements make it quite difficult for the state to deprive a citizen of his or her liberty or property.

This thinking reflects the inherent liberalism of Anglo-American criminal law that was captured by Sir William Blackstone in his oft-quoted statement that "the law holds, that it is better that ten guilty persons escape, than that one innocent suffer,"[12] and that is echoed in the U.S. Supreme Court's declarations that "[t]he principle that there is a presumption of innocence in favor of the accused is the undoubted law, axiomatic and elementary, and its enforcement lies at the foundation of the administration of our criminal law"[13] and that

> use of the reasonable-doubt standard is indispensable to command the respect and confidence of the community in applications of the criminal law. It is critical that the moral force of the criminal law not be diluted by a standard of proof that leaves people in doubt whether innocent men are being condemned. It is also important in our free society that every individual going about his ordinary affairs have confidence that his government cannot adjudge him guilty of a criminal offense without convincing a proper fact finder of his guilt with utmost certainty.[14]

Other procedural safeguards evolved as well, two of which—the common law attorney-client privilege,[15] and the Fifth Amendment right not to be compelled to be a witness against oneself[16]—are particularly relevant to the present consideration. Both of these provisions protect individual liberty by creating obstacles to criminal conviction. Both place accurate and potentially incriminating information beyond the reach of the prosecutor. The former creates a zone of privacy within which individuals may impart information to their counsel for the purpose of receiving legal advice without thereby manufacturing evidence against themselves. The latter ensures that the state honor the requirement of the presumption of innocence by "forc[ing] the government not only to establish its case, but to do so by its own resources. It prohibits the state from easing its burden of proof by simply calling the defendant as its witness and forcing him to make the prosecution's case."[17] By placing the techniques of the Inquisition and the Star Chamber beyond the reach of the state, the right against self-incrimination embodies the most significant protection of individual liberty bequeathed to us by the common law.[18]

These seven features—(1) the *mens rea* requirement, (2) the absence of vicarious criminal liability, (3) the principle of legality, (4) the presumption of innocence, (5) the requirement of proof beyond reasonable doubt, (6) the attorney-client privilege, and (7) the privilege against self-incrimination—reflect the inherent liberalism of American criminal law at the dawn of the 20th century. This liberalism, which bestowed the benefit of protection against governmental overreaching upon individuals, was not without cost, however. By making it more difficult for the prosecution to obtain convictions, the liberal features of the criminal law reduced its deterrent value and thereby reduced its effectiveness in suppressing crime. Thus, Anglo-American criminal law purchased individuals' protection against erroneous or abusive governmental action at the cost of individuals' reduced protection against the criminal activity of their fellows.

In the context of white-collar crime, the cost imposed by the liberal features of the criminal law is especially high. To see why, imagine what the position of a federal prosecutor charged with combating white-collar crime would be if he or she were burdened with the substantive and procedural safeguards of the traditional criminal law. First, consider the effect that the presumption of innocence and the requirement of proof beyond reasonable doubt would have on the prosecutor's efforts. Like all real-world prosecutors, our imaginary one would be acutely aware of the limitations on his or her investigative and prosecutorial resources. Policing all of the business concerns in the United States not only for honest dealing but also for compliance with the myriad regulations that carry criminal penalties is a truly monumental task. No matter how large the Department of Justice's budget for white-collar crime may be, it would still be insufficient to address anything beyond the tip of the iceberg of potential offenses. Furthermore, white-collar crime is typically characterized by deceptive behavior. There is usually no *corpus delicti* or "smoking gun" to introduce into evidence. White-collar criminal activity is intentionally designed to be indistinguishable from non-criminal activity. As a result, considerable investigation may be required merely to establish that a crime has been committed. Even then, unraveling the deception may require a great deal of legal or accounting sophistication, or both. Under these circumstances, compliance with procedural rules that require "the government not only to establish its case, but to do so by its own resources"[19] can be an extremely expensive proposition. The assets that our imaginary prosecutor must expend to satisfy such liberal safeguards in each case that he or she brings greatly reduce the total number of cases that he or she can afford to bring. This situation, in turn, significantly reduces the deterrent value of the statutes that the prosecutor is charged with enforcing. Thus, in the context of white-collar crime, the law enforcement costs of the presumption of innocence and the requirement of proof beyond reasonable doubt are inordinately high.

Next, consider the burden the *mens rea* requirement places on our prosecutor in the absence of vicarious criminal liability. Without vicarious liability, he or she could prosecute individuals only for offenses they personally commit. Thus, in order to obtain a conviction, the prosecutor would have to establish that the individual defendant acted with the requisite *mens rea*, which means proving that the defendant intentionally or recklessly engaged in or authorized dishonest business practices or the violation of regulations. When an individual acts alone or with a small number of confederates, this requirement may not present an inordinate problem. In the corporate context, however, evidence of *mens rea* can be difficult, and in some cases impossible, to obtain. It is in the nature of the corporate form to diffuse decisionmaking responsibility. Decisions made by one member of a firm may not be fully informed by what other members of the firm are doing or have decided. As the courts have noted, "[c]orporations compartmentalize knowledge, subdividing the elements of specific duties and operations into smaller components."[20] Furthermore, corporations frequently take actions that were never explicitly known to, or authorized by, any identifiable individual or individuals within the firm. "Complex business structures, characterized by decentralization and delegation of authority, commonly adopted by corporations for business purposes, make it difficult to identify the particular corporate agents responsible for . . . violations."[21] Accordingly, without vicarious criminal liability, the *mens rea* requirement will often present our hypothetical prosecutor with an insurmountable barrier to successful prosecutions.

The principle of legality can also pose special problems for our prosecutor's efforts. Legality requires both that criminal offenses be defined clearly enough to give citizens adequate warning of what conduct is prohibited and that criminal statutes be narrowly construed. The problem this causes is that the more definite the law is as to what conduct is prohibited, the more guidance it provides to what former Chief Justice Burger referred to as "the ever-inventive American 'con artist' "[22] to come up with "new varieties of fraud"[23] that are not technically illegal. Further, because the rule of lenity requires the narrow construction of criminal statutes, it creates loopholes in the fabric of the law against deceptive and fraudulent conduct through which these con artists can squeeze dishonest practices.[24] This construction results in a running battle between those who would exploit the loopholes and Congress, which must continually pass new, specific legislation to close them.[25] Meanwhile, many forms of dishonest or deceptive behavior would remain beyond the reach of our imaginary prosecutor.

The greatest challenge our prosecutor would face, however, is likely to be presented by the attorney-client privilege and the right against self-incrimination. As noted above, because white-collar crime consists primarily of crimes of deception,[26] the type of physical evidence associated with traditional criminal activity is rarely available. The evidence on which conviction for a white-collar offense must rest will be almost entirely documentary in nature and will consist predominantly of the business records of the firm that the defendant works for. But to the extent that these records are in the personal possession of the defendant, contain communications between the defendant or other members of the firm and corporate counsel, or are the work product of corporate counsel, the right against self-incrimination and the attorney-client privilege render them unavailable to the prosecution. To a much greater extent than is the case with regard to traditional criminal activity, the evidence necessary for a conviction for a white-collar criminal offense will be in the hands of those who cannot be compelled to produce it. This situation once again places our beleaguered prosecutor in an unenviable position.

Viewed from the perspective of the early 20th century, these four problems—limited investigative and prosecutorial resources, the difficulty of establishing *mens rea*, the loopholes created by narrowly construed statutes, and the difficulty of obtaining necessary documentary evidence—would constitute the chief impediments to the effective enforcement of white-collar criminal statutes. For the federal government to mount a successful campaign to suppress such crime, the criminal law would have to evolve ways to overcome these problems. And that is precisely what happened. To overcome the problem of limited police resources, the law evolved so as to conscript businesses and businesspeople into the role of deputy law enforcement agents. To overcome the difficulty of establishing *mens rea*, the law evolved to allow punishment in the absence of proof of intentional wrongdoing by specific individuals. To overcome the problem of statutory loopholes, the law evolved broader, inchoate versions of traditional offenses and entirely new ''secondary'' offenses.[27] And to overcome the difficulty of obtaining necessary documentary evidence, the law evolved mechanisms for circumventing common law and constitutional privileges.

There were three main vehicles for the evolution of these solutions: (1) the concept of corporate criminal responsibility, (2) the legislative creation of new offenses, and (3) the U.S. Sentencing Commission's Sentencing Guidelines for Organizations.[28] In the remaining three chapters of Part I, I propose to examine each of these vehicles and to show how each eases the burden on the prosecution. In doing so, however, I must ask for the reader's indulgence. To fully explain these legal developments, I must go into considerable, and perhaps to some extent arcane, detail. This does not make for the most scintillating reading. However, if the reader will bear with me for the next three chapters, I promise to redeem his or her patience in what follows. In Part II, I will show how these developments create exceedingly difficult dilemmas for ethically conscientious businesspeople and yield what may be quite surprising answers to the quiz in the opening pages of this book.

4. The Solutions—Corporate Criminal Responsibility

Corporations, like all businesses, are abstract entities. They have no minds in which to form intentions, no hearts in which to conceive a guilty will, and no bodies that can be imprisoned or corporeally punished in response to bad behavior. They have no actual existence apart from the human beings of which they are comprised. How then can corporations be subject to criminal punishment in contradistinction to (and often in addition to) their individual members? How can there be corporate as opposed to individual criminal responsibility?

That was the question confronting the Supreme Court in 1909 when it decided *New York Central & Hudson River Railroad Co. v. United States.*[1] In that case, an assistant manager of the railroad company had given illegal rebates in contravention of the Elkins Act.[2] Both the manager and the railroad company were convicted of violating the act.[3] The railroad appealed its conviction, arguing that holding the corporation liable both violated the presumption of innocence of the directors and shareholders of the company, and improperly imposed vicarious criminal liability on the shareholders who were innocent of wrongdoing.[4]

In addressing those contentions, the Court recognized that under the doctrine of *respondeat superior* corporations could be held liable in tort for the actions of their agents taken within the scope of their employment.[5] The Court found that such vicarious liability was justified not "because the principal actually participates in the malice or fraud, but because the act is done for the benefit of the principal . . . and justice requires that the latter shall be held responsible for damages to the individual who has suffered by such conduct."[6] The Court then proceeded to "go only a step farther" and, "in the interest of public policy," permit corporations to be held criminally liable for the actions of their agents as well.[7] The Court was quite explicit in identifying the public policy interest that required such an expansion of the doctrine of *respondeat superior*, declaring that if "corporations may not be held responsible for and charged with the knowledge and purposes of their agents, . . . many offenses might go unpunished."[8] Thus,

> [w]hile the law should have regard to the rights of all, and to those of corporations no less than to those of individuals, it cannot shut its eyes to the fact that the great majority of business transactions in modern times are conducted through these bodies, and particularly that interstate commerce is almost entirely in their hands, and to give them immunity from all punishment because of the old and exploded doctrine that a corporation cannot commit a crime would virtually take away the only means of effectually controlling the subject-matter and correcting the abuses aimed at.[9]

This constitutes a fairly direct statement that the liberal protections of the presumption of innocence and the ban on vicarious criminal liability must be overridden because federal statutes aimed at the suppression of white-collar crime would otherwise be unenforceable.

The Ninth Circuit Court of Appeals applied the same rationale 61 years later when it decided *United States v. Hilton Hotels Corp.*[10] In that case, one of the hotel chain's purchasing agents threatened to withhold the hotel's business from a supplier in contravention of the Sherman Act[11] despite such action being against the hotel's official policy and despite the purchasing agent having been given explicit instructions not to engage in such conduct.[12] The court nevertheless held the corporation liable "for the acts of its agents in the scope of their employment, even though contrary to general corporate policy and express instructions to the agent."[13] The court justified this apparently inescapable form of vicarious liability on the ground that

> [c]omplex business structures, characterized by decentralization and delegation of authority, commonly adopted by corporations for business purposes, make it difficult to identify the particular corporate agents responsible for Sherman Act violations. . . .
>
> In sum, identification of the particular agents responsible for a Sherman Act violation is especially difficult, and their conviction and punishment is peculiarly ineffective as a deterrent. At the same time, conviction and punishment of the business entity itself is likely to be both appropriate and effective.[14]

Once again, this statement constitutes a rather frank admission that vicarious criminal liability is necessary for the effective enforcement of federal statutes designed to regulate business behavior.

Although corporations are thus criminally responsible for the actions of all of their employees taken within the scope of their employment, corporate criminal responsibility is not limited to such cases. As pointed out in *United States v. Bank of New England*,[15] corporations are also criminally responsible for the collective actions of all of their employees.[16] In *Bank of New England*, the bank was convicted of violating the Currency Transaction Reporting Act[17] for failing to file the required reports when one of the bank's customers made several withdrawals that collectively totaled more than $10,000.[18] The bank appealed a jury instruction equating the bank's knowledge with "the sum of the knowledge of all of the employees."[19] The trial judge instructed the jury that,

> if Employee A knows one facet of the currency reporting requirement, B knows another facet of it, and C a third facet of it, the bank knows them all. So if you find that an employee within the scope of his employment knew that CTRs had to be filed, even if multiple checks are used, the bank is deemed to know it. The bank is also deemed to know it if each of several employees knew a part of that requirement and the sum of what the separate employees knew amounted to knowledge that such a requirement existed.[20]

The court upheld this instruction as proper, stating that

> A collective knowledge instruction is entirely appropriate in the context of corporate criminal liability. The acts of a corporation are, after all, simply the acts of all of its employees operating within the scope of their employment. . . . Corporations compartmentalize knowledge, subdividing the elements of specific duties and operations into smaller components. The aggregate of those components constitutes the corporation's knowledge of a particular operation. It is irrelevant whether employees administering one component of an operation know the specific activities of employees administering another aspect of the operation. . . . ["T]he corporation is considered to have acquired the collective knowledge of its employees and is held responsible for their failure to act accordingly.["][21]

25

Therefore, a corporation can be guilty of an offense even though no individual member of the firm has committed any crime. Such a result is difficult to explain on any basis other than the absolute necessity of vicarious criminal liability to the effectiveness of the regulatory legislation.

Consider the extent to which this conception of corporate criminal responsibility solves our hypothetical prosecutor's problems. In the first place, it eases his or her struggle with limited resources by shifting a significant portion of the cost of crime prevention from the government to the corporations themselves. Under the rules of *New York Central* and *Hilton Hotels*, the only way for a firm to avoid criminal liability is to constantly monitor the behavior of all of its employees to ensure that none of them intentionally or recklessly violates the law.[22] Actual monitoring is required because merely having corporate policies or issuing explicit instructions against violating the law are not sufficient to protect the firm from conviction. Furthermore, under the rule of *Bank of New England*, firms must continually review all corporate activities to ensure that no laws are unintentionally violated as a result of the ill-informed or poorly coordinated actions of the companies' various employees. Thus, this conception of corporate criminal responsibility goes a long way toward enlisting corporations as deputy law enforcement agencies.

This form of corporate criminal responsibility also helps the prosecutor overcome the problem posed by the *mens rea* requirement. Even under the doctrine of *respondeat superior*, the prosecutor would still have to present evidence proving that at least one employee intentionally or recklessly violated the law—something that can be difficult to do in the corporate context.[23] But *Bank of New England*'s collective knowledge doctrine frees the prosecutor from this constraint. Because the corporation will be deemed to have the sum total of the knowledge of all of its employees, the prosecutor need only prove that it was possible for the corporation to assemble the required knowledge to establish corporate *mens rea*. As a *scienter* requirement, this borders on the oxymoronic because it implies that a company that does not have knowledge in fact, and that is not even negligent in failing to assemble it, can nevertheless act knowingly. But it has the prosecutorial virtue of converting unintentional individual conduct into intentional corporate conduct. Thus, by relieving the prosecutor of the burden of proving intent, this conception of corporate criminal responsibility eliminates one of the major hurdles to the successful prosecution of white-collar offenses.

Finally, the ability to hold businesses vicariously liable for the offenses of their employees helps our prosecutor overcome the impediment that the Fifth Amendment privilege against self-incrimination poses to his or her efforts to obtain evidence. To see how, consider that in the 1906 case of *Hale v. Henkel*,[24] the Supreme Court held that the Fifth Amendment privilege did not apply to corporations. This decision was perfectly sensible at the time, coming as it did three years before *New York Central* when corporations were not subject to criminal punishment. After all, what would be the point in holding that an entity that could not be prosecuted had a right against self-incrimination? The situation changed when, three years later, corporations became liable to the criminal sanction. The point of extending the Fifth Amendment privilege to corporations then became precisely the same as it is with regard to individuals: to preserve the liberal character of the criminal law embodied in the presumption of innocence that "prohibits the state from easing its burden of proof by simply calling the defendant as its witness and forcing him to make the prosecution's case."[25] The Court, however, never revisited the issue with this purpose in mind, but simply continued to cite *Hale* for what became known as the collective entity rule—the proposition that "for purposes of the Fifth Amendment, corporations and other collective entities are treated differently from individuals."[26]

The advent of corporate criminal responsibility, then, created a new class of defendant shorn of the right against self-incrimination. This consequence was a boon to white-collar prosecutors in two ways. First, in cases against corporate defendants, prosecutors could subpoena whatever documentary evidence they desired without fear that the subpoena would be resisted on Fifth Amendment grounds. Second, in cases against individual defendants employed by corporations or other collective entities, prosecutors could circumvent the defendants' personal Fifth Amendment rights by issuing subpoenas to them in their corporate capacity. By issuing a subpoena to John Doe, employee of ABC Corporation, rather than merely to John Doe in his personal capacity, prosecutors could compel an individual to produce corporate documents that would be used as evidence against him personally. As the Court explained, "[t]he plain mandate of these decisions is that without regard to whether the subpoena is addressed to the corporation, or . . . to the individual in his capacity as a custodian, a corporate custodian . . . may not resist a subpoena for corporate records on Fifth Amendment grounds."[27] Indeed, the Court was quite explicit in its rationale for thus limiting the scope of the Fifth Amendment privilege: such an interpretation was necessary for the effective enforcement of the statutes directed against white-collar crime.

> We note further that recognizing a Fifth Amendment privilege on behalf of the records custodians of collective entities would have a detrimental impact on the Government's efforts to prosecute "white-collar crime," one of the most serious problems confronting law enforcement authorities. "The greater portion of evidence of wrongdoing by an organization or its representatives is usually found in the official records and documents of that organization. Were the cloak of the privilege to be thrown around these impersonal records and documents, effective enforcement of many federal and state laws would be impossible."[28]

There should be nothing surprising about the evolution of corporate criminal responsibility, and I am certainly not suggesting that there was any nefarious agency at work in its development. Rather, the current conception of corporate criminal responsibility should be seen as the logical outgrowth of the effort to police the business environment for honest dealing and regulatory violations. For the federal government to wage a successful campaign against white-collar crime, it had to find a way to circumvent the features that arise from the civil libertarian features inherent in the traditional criminal law. The conception of corporate criminal responsibility that developed in the context of that campaign is well designed to serve that end. It reverses the presumption of innocence by conclusively presuming the firm to be guilty not only of any crime committed by its individual employees in the scope of their employment, but also of any crime that *could have been* committed if the firm had assembled the requisite collective knowledge, whether or not it did so. This advances the campaign against white-collar crime by shifting a large amount of the costs of both crime prevention and investigation from the government to businesses, which can now avoid criminal liability only by continually monitoring the behavior of its individual employees and by auditing the diverse particles of information possessed by each. Corporate criminal responsibility also eliminates the burden of establishing corporate *mens rea* in the form of a collective, corporate intention to engage in criminal activity by imputing the intention of any of its agents to the corporation even when the agent is acting contrary to corporate policy or instructions, and by converting the unintentional and uncoordinated actions of the firm's individual employees into the intentional action of the firm. And finally, because businesses have no Fifth Amendment right against self-incrimination, corporate criminal responsibility opens the door to evidence that would otherwise be constitutionally unavailable to prosecutors.

5. The Solutions—New Offenses

Even with the advantages of corporate criminal responsibility, a federal prosecutor engaged in the campaign against white-collar crime would still face an uphill battle. Traditional criminal law required that criminal offenses be defined with sufficient clarity to put the ordinary person on notice as to what conduct was prohibited. But in the context of white-collar crime, which consists primarily of crimes of deception, such clarity would instruct criminals in the best way to skirt the law. In cases involving deception, proving every element of an offense, especially *mens rea*, beyond reasonable doubt would be a very arduous task. To wage a successful war on white-collar crime, a federal prosecutor would need more weapons than the criminal law traditionally provides.

Those weapons arrived in the form of the legislative creation and expansive judicial interpretation of new criminal offenses.[1] Specifically, Congress passed, and the federal courts endorsed, criminal statutes creating offenses of broad scope, or with reduced *mens rea* requirements, or that consisted entirely of actions that make it more difficult for the government to prosecute other substantive offenses. Each type of new offense made the life of a federal prosecutor considerably easier.

Consider first the broadly defined substantive offenses; the various federal fraud statutes and the Racketeer Influenced and Corrupt Organization Act (RICO)[2] can serve as useful examples. Mail fraud,[3] which is probably the archetypal white-collar criminal offense, has already been mentioned.[4] The traditional conception of criminal fraud consisted of one party obtaining the property of another on the basis of an intentional misrepresentation of a material fact upon which the victim relied.[5] This required the prosecution to establish that (1) the defendant had obtained the property of another, (2) the defendant had knowingly made a false representation of fact, (3) the fact was material, and (4) the victim relied on the false representation in transferring the property. The federal mail fraud statute, in contrast, covers any scheme or artifice to defraud that involves the use of the mails. To establish a scheme or artifice to defraud, the prosecution is required to prove only that the defendant participated in "any deliberate plan of action or course of conduct by which someone intends to deceive or to cheat another of something of value."[6] The prosecution need not prove that the scheme was designed to obtain the property of another because the statute defines a scheme or artifice to defraud to include "a scheme or artifice to deprive another of the intangible right of honest services."[7] It need prove neither that the defendant actually obtained the property of the victim or deprived the victim of the intangible right of honest services nor that the victim relied on any representation of the defendant because "[b]y prohibiting the 'scheme to defraud,' rather than the completed fraud, the elements of reliance and damage would clearly be inconsistent with the statutes Congress enacted."[8] Thus, "[t]he common-law requirements of 'justifiable reliance' and 'damages' . . . plainly have no place in the federal fraud statutes."[9] And finally, the prosecution need not prove that there was a misrepresentation of fact because,

> under the mail fraud statute, it is just as unlawful to speak "half truths" or to omit to state facts necessary to make the statements made, in light of the circumstances under which they were made, not misleading. The statements need not be false or fraudulent on their face, and the accused need not misrepresent any fact, since all that is necessary is that the scheme be reasonably calculated to deceive persons of ordinary prudence and comprehension.[10]

To describe the scope of the mail fraud statute as broad may be a bit of an understatement. Indeed, the Second Circuit Court of Appeals recently declared that "the potential reach of [the mail fraud statute] is virtually limitless,"[11] pointing out that,

> a customer who importunes an employee to allow her to use the company's telephone access code to make an important long-distance telephone call, in the face of a written company policy expressly prohibiting non-employees from using the access code, could conceivably fall within the scope of the statute if read literally. So too could an employee's use of his company's letterhead to lend authority to a letter of complaint mailed to the employee's landlord in disregard of the company's code of conduct prohibiting the use of the company's letterhead for non-company business.[12]

Thus, in addition to the cases already mentioned in which the government brought mail fraud charges against a developer who falsely claimed its homes were good investments,[13] and a physician who failed to disclose to his patients that he received a fee for referring them to a hospital,[14] the government has brought charges against a county commissioner who threatened to distribute a compromising videotape of a candidate for another seat on the board,[15] a man who secretly lobbied his brother—a U.S. senator—on behalf of a corporation,[16] and an IRS employee who looked at confidential tax returns in contravention of IRS policy.[17]

Perhaps the best illustration of the breadth of the federal fraud statutes is the recent prosecution of Martha Stewart. Prosecutors charged Stewart with securities fraud for publicly and falsely asserting her innocence of trading stocks on nonpublic information.[18] Stewart, who sold her shares of ImClone stock immediately before a sharp decline in its price, publicly asserted that she did so in response to a preestablished stop-loss order rather than because of a tip from her broker based on nonpublic information.[19] Arguing that "Martha Stewart's reputation, as well as the likelihood of any criminal or regulatory action against Stewart, were material to Martha Stewart Living Omnimedia, Inc. ("MSLO") shareholders because of the negative impact that any such action or damage to her reputation could have on the company which bears her name,"[20] the government charged Stewart with securities fraud for attempting to

> stop or at least slow the steady erosion of MSLO's stock price caused by investor concerns [by making or causing] to be made a series of false and misleading public statements during June 2002 regarding her sale of ImClone stock on December 27, 2001, that concealed that Stewart had been provided [nonpublic] information . . . and that Stewart had sold her ImClone stock while in possession of that information.[21]

The government brought this indictment against Stewart despite the fact that it did not charge her with insider trading. Thus, the scope of the securities fraud statute is sufficiently broad to allow the indictment of high-profile corporate executives for publicly declaring their innocence of offenses that they are not even charged with committing. From this example, one can see why the former chief of Business Frauds Prosecution for the Southern District of New York would declare that "[t]o federal prosecutors of white collar crime, the mail fraud statute is our Stradivarius, our Colt 45, our Louisville Slugger, our Cuisinart—and our true love."[22]

Similarly, RICO creates federal offenses not known to the common law that significantly extend the reach of federal prosecutors. RICO criminalizes the direct or indirect investment in, acquisition or maintenance of an interest in, or participation in the affairs of an enterprise that is engaged in or affects interstate or foreign commerce through a pattern of racketeering activity, which is defined as the commission of two or more predicate offenses during a period of 10 years.[23] It also criminalizes the conspiracy to engage in such prohibited activity.[24] Furthermore, the predicate offenses constitute an extremely wide array of both state and federal offenses, including the opened-ended federal fraud statutes just discussed.[25] These provisions give federal prosecutors the power to go after virtually any form of group activity that involves the commission of, or merely the plans to commit, more than one criminal offense.

In passing RICO, Congress was explicit that the statute's purpose was to enhance federal law enforcement power, stating in its findings that it enacted the statute to remedy

> defects in the evidence-gathering process of the law inhibiting the development of the legally admissible evidence necessary to bring criminal and other sanctions or remedies to bear on the unlawful activities of those engaged in organized crime and because the sanctions and remedies available to the Government are unnecessarily limited in scope and impact.[26]

Indeed, Congress gave the courts explicit instructions to construe the statute broadly by including a provision that specifically calls for a liberal construction of RICO.[27] The Supreme Court has heeded those instructions, stating that "RICO is to be read broadly. This is the lesson not only of Congress's self-consciously expansive language and overall approach, but also of its express admonition that RICO is to 'be liberally construed to effectuate its remedial purposes.'"[28] Accordingly, the Court held that RICO's application was not limited to the efforts of organized crime to infiltrate legitimate businesses but may also be used against any association of individuals that pursues criminal purposes.[29] Thus, "RICO's versatility has allowed RICO prosecutions for tax, securities, commodities, and bankruptcy fraud as well as for obscenity, drug, or gambling violations."[30]

Next, consider the myriad new regulatory offenses that require either no or a reduced level of *mens rea*. Traditionally, criminal law required either intentional or reckless conduct to sustain a conviction for a crime. There was no strict liability at common law,[31] and many jurisdictions did not permit criminal convictions for negligent behavior.[32] Among those that did, ordinary civil negligence could not sustain a criminal conviction.[33] A more culpable form of negligence, criminal negligence, was required. Criminal negligence requires that "the negligence of the accused must be 'culpable,' 'gross,' or 'reckless,' that is, the conduct of the accused must be such a departure from what would be the conduct of an ordinary prudent or careful man under the same circumstances as to be incompatible with a proper regard for human life, or conduct amounting to an indifference to the consequences."[34]

This situation changed over the course of the 20th century as Congress enacted regulatory statutes that created criminal offenses requiring no *mens rea*, and the courts upheld the legitimacy of these "public welfare offenses."[35] In doing so, the Supreme Court recognized that Congress was enacting "increasingly numerous and detailed regulations which heighten the duties of those in control of particular industries, trades, properties or activities that affect public health, safety or welfare,"[36] the violation of which "impairs the efficiency of controls deemed essential to the social order as presently constituted."[37] Because, with regard to such regulations, "whatever the intent of the violator, the injury is the same, and the consequences are injurious or not according to fortuity,"[38] the Court endorsed "construing statutes and regulations which make no mention of intent as dispensing with it and holding that the guilty act alone makes out the crime."[39] Thus, just as it did in recognizing corporate criminal responsibility, the Court justified relaxing one of the liberal features of the traditional criminal law, the *mens rea* requirement, on the ground that doing so was necessary to effectively police the business environment.

Under the public welfare offense doctrine, businesses and individuals can be criminally punished for entirely innocent regulatory violations, at least when the potential penalty is relatively small.[40] For example, a company that operated a tank farm near Boston Harbor was convicted of violating the Refuse Act[41] when it allowed oil to seep into a part of the harbor, despite the fact that the government made no allegation of a lack of care by the company, and that the company "immediately undertook to clean up the oil and to trace its source . . . [and] worked diligently to divert or drain the accumulation."[42] Once again, the result was justified on the ground of law enforcement considerations.[43]

> Merely to attempt to formulate, let alone apply, [a *mens rea* requirement] would be to risk crippling the Refuse Act as an enforcement tool. . . . [I]t would be difficult indeed, and to no purpose, for the government to have to take issue with elaborate factual and theoretical arguments concerning who, why and what went wrong. . . . In the present circumstances we see no unfairness in predicating liability on actual non-compliance rather than either intentions or best efforts.[44]

In addition to public welfare offenses, Congress authorized and the courts endorsed the imposition of substantial criminal punishment for regulatory violations resulting from ordinary, as opposed to criminal, negligence. This development has allowed the criminal prosecution not only of employees who are themselves negligent, but also of their supervisors. Thus, a roadmaster employed by a railway company to oversee the maintenance and construction of the track was sentenced to six months in prison, six months in a halfway house, six months of supervised release, and a $5,000 fine for violating the Clean Water Act[45] when a backhoe operator on his crew negligently pierced an oil pipeline, causing a discharge of oil into a nearby river.[46] The roadmaster, who was charged in keeping with "the stated policy of prosecutors in the past several administrations to seek to hold liable the highest level culpable officials of an entity that commits [white-collar] criminal violations,"[47] appealed, arguing that the government had to prove criminal, rather than ordinary, negligence. The court rejected this argument, noting that "[i]t is well established that a public welfare statute may subject a person to criminal liability for his or her ordinary negligence without violating due process."[48]

Finally, consider the recent creation of new "secondary" offenses, which consist entirely of actions that make it more difficult for the government to prosecute other substantive criminal offenses. Traditionally, criminal offenses consisted of actions that either directly harmed or violated the rights of others or that were immoral in themselves. But as the campaign against white-collar crime evolved, so too did offenses that consist of conduct that is perfectly innocent in itself but that impedes or fails to aid the government's efforts to prosecute white-collar crime.

As a first example, consider currency reporting and money laundering offenses. Currency reporting offenses consist of the failure of financial institutions and other covered businesses to report transactions involving more than $10,000 to the federal government.[49] Although there is nothing illegal about engaging in a financial transaction involving more than $10,000, the government can use this information to help it identify those parties that may be engaging in criminal activity. By criminalizing the failure to report such information to the government, the currency reporting statutes essentially make it a crime not to aid federal law enforcement efforts.

Federal money laundering statutes criminalize the otherwise legal use of money obtained through criminal activity. According to 18 U.S.C. § 1956, it is illegal to engage in any financial transactions with the proceeds of unlawful activity with the knowledge that the transaction is intended to conceal information about the funds.[50] The courts have interpreted the language of this statute to mean that purchasing just about anything with money known to be the proceeds of unlawful activity will constitute a transaction designed to conceal information about the funds. Thus, in *United States v. Jackson*,[51] the Court of Appeals for the Seventh Circuit upheld the money laundering conviction of an alleged drug dealer for writing checks to purchase cell phones and pay his rent, and for cashing checks for small amounts at his local bank.[52]

Furthermore, 18 U.S.C. § 1957 makes it illegal to engage in monetary transactions of more than $10,000 involving the proceeds of unlawful activity, regardless of the purpose for which the transaction is undertaken.[53] Several federal circuits have interpreted this statute to cover the withdrawal of more than $10,000 from any account that contains at least $10,000 in unlawful proceeds, regardless of how much untainted money the accounts also contain.[54] This provision criminalizes the use of more than $10,000 of one's own money, regardless of its source, once it has been commingled with illegal proceeds. The breadth of this statute is so great that it had to be amended in 1988 to permit criminal defendants to pay their attorneys.[55] By thus making the otherwise innocent use of illegal proceeds a criminal offense in itself, the money laundering statutes expand the range of activities the government may investigate by an order of magnitude and greatly facilitate the government's ability to trace suspected criminal activity. In essence, these statutes make it a crime to make it more difficult for the government to detect one's crimes.[56]

A second example of the new secondary offenses is the crime of making false statements to federal investigators. Under 18 U.S.C. § 1001, it is a felony to lie to or to otherwise deceptively conceal material information from officials investigating any matter within the jurisdiction of the federal government. This offense may be committed whenever an individual responds to a question from a federal investigator, regardless of whether he or she is under oath. Under § 1001, simply to deny one's guilt of an offense can be a crime. For example, in 1998 a union official was convicted not only of accepting unlawful cash payments but also of making a false statement for responding "no" when two FBI agents came to the man's home and asked him whether he had received such payments.[57] In upholding the official's conviction for making a false statement, the Supreme Court was clear about the breadth of the statute's application, stating, "[b]y its terms, 18 U.S.C. § 1001 covers 'any' false statement—that is, a false statement 'of whatever kind.' The word 'no' in response to a question assuredly makes a 'statement.'" Indeed, in rejecting the union official's argument that an exception must be made for an "exculpatory no," the Court explicitly recognized the power § 1001 places in the hands of federal prosecutors by stating,

> Petitioner repeats the argument made by many supporters of the "exculpatory no," that the doctrine is necessary to eliminate the grave risk that § 1001 will become an instrument of prosecutorial abuse. The supposed danger is that overzealous prosecutors will use this provision as a means of "piling on" offenses—sometimes punishing the denial of wrongdoing more severely than the wrongdoing itself. The objectors' principal grievance on this score, however, lies not with the hypothetical prosecutors but with Congress itself, which has decreed the obstruction of a legitimate investigation to be a separate offense, and a serious one.[58]

A final example of this type of offense can be supplied by the statutes prohibiting obstruction of justice.[59] 18 U.S.C. §§ 1503 and 1505 prohibit any efforts to corruptly influence, obstruct, or impede any federal judicial or administrative proceeding or legislative inquiry. In addition, 18 U.S.C. §§ 1512, 1519, and 1520 prohibit any efforts to corruptly (or, in the case of § 1519, merely knowingly) alter, destroy, mutilate, or conceal documents or other objects that might be relevant to any official proceeding or investigation of any federal department or agency.

The power and broad reach of these statutes are illustrated by the recent convictions of the Arthur Andersen accounting firm and Frank Quattrone, the high-profile investment banker for Credit Suisse First Boston Corporation. Andersen, which was the accounting firm employed to audit Enron's books, was never charged with or convicted of any fraudulent practices or accounting irregularities. Rather, the company was indicted for corruptly persuading and attempting to persuade its employees to alter and destroy documents related to a Securities and Exchange Commission investigation of Enron's special purpose entities.[60] Andersen was convicted of violating § 1512 solely on the basis of in-house counsel Nancy Temple's response to a *draft* memorandum concerning Andersen's actions in response to an Enron press release characterizing certain losses as nonrecurring. The obstruction consisted of Temple's recommendation to delete "some language that might suggest we have concluded the release is misleading . . . [when] in fact Andersen had concluded that the term 'non-recurring' was misleading."[61] Similarly, Quattrone, who was not charged with any substantive fraud, was convicted on three counts of obstruction of justice and sentenced to 18 months in prison for forwarding another employee's e-mail suggesting that Credit Suisse First Boston Corporation's employees comply with the company's document retention policy and "catch up on file cleaning" with an added injunction: "having been a key witness in a securities litigation case in south texas [sic] i [sic] strongly advise you to follow these procedures."[62]

Clearly, false statements and obstruction of justice are offenses designed to aid federal law enforcement efforts. Both offenses make it a separate crime for an individual to do anything that would make the government's effort to convict that individual or anyone else of another substantive crime more difficult. Neither offense, however, requires that there actually be any underlying substantive criminal activity. One can be guilty of either offense without being guilty of anything else, as Martha Stewart's recent convictions demonstrate. Stewart was convicted of both false statements and obstruction of justice in connection with statements she made to federal investigators during a Securities and Exchange Commission investigation of allegations of insider trading in shares of ImClone Systems Inc. stock. Stewart was never charged with insider trading, and, in fact, could not be because she was not an ImClone insider, she was not tipped by such an insider, and she did not breach any fiduciary duty to the source of the information, who was her broker and who recommended the trade to her.[63] Nevertheless, Stewart was charged with and convicted of making false statements and of obstructing an agency investigation by providing a false account of the communications she had with her broker concerning the sale of her stock.[64] Thus, these statutes empower prosecutors to go after not just criminals attempting to avoid detection and punishment, but anyone who interferes with a federal investigation, regardless of the reason.

The creation of these new offenses went a long way toward relieving the burden that the inherent liberalism of the traditional criminal law would have otherwise placed on federal prosecutors. In the first place, the enactment of broadly defined substantive offenses such as mail and wire fraud and of RICO greatly ameliorated the inconveniences arising from the requirement of the principle of legality that criminal offenses be clearly defined and narrowly construed. As a feature of the common law, the principle of legality may be overridden by statute as long as the legislation is not unconstitutionally vague. Thus, Congress's enactment of expansive, somewhat amorphous new offenses like the federal fraud offenses and RICO, coupled with specific injunctions to the courts to construe the offenses broadly, constituted an effective means for closing the loopholes in the fabric of white-collar criminal law.

That is certainly the way the mail and wire fraud statutes have been used. As described by former Chief Justice Warren Burger, the mail fraud statute

> has traditionally been used against fraudulent activity as a first line of defense. When a "new" fraud develops—as constantly happens—the mail fraud statute becomes a stopgap device to deal on a temporary basis with the new phenomenon, until particularized legislation can be developed and passed to deal directly with the evil.[65]

Amplifying this sentiment, one federal prosecutor explained that

> the mail fraud statute, together with its lineal descendant, the wire fraud statute, has been characterized as the "first

line of defense" against virtually every new area of fraud to develop in the United States in the past century. Its applications, too numerous to catalog, cover not only the full range of consumer frauds, stock frauds, land frauds, bank frauds, insurance frauds, and commodity frauds, but have extended even to such areas as blackmail, counterfeiting, election fraud, and bribery. In many of these and other areas, where legislatures have sometimes been slow to enact specific prohibitory legislation, the mail fraud statute has frequently represented the sole instrument of justice that could be wielded against the ever-innovative practitioners of deceit.[66]

Thus, statutes such as the mail and wire fraud statutes are a manifestation of Congress's quest for the ultimate weapon in the battle between con artists' efforts to skate along the edge of the law and the federal government's effort to eliminate dishonest or deceptive business practices.

The cost of creating offenses that are broad enough to reach the full range of deceptive activity, however, is paid in terms of the failure to furnish the public with clear notice as to what constitutes criminal conduct and the lack of definite guidelines to govern law enforcement. Although the courts have not (or perhaps simply have not yet)[67] declared the federal fraud statutes to be unconstitutionally vague, many have recognized that they tread uncomfortably close to the constitutional border. In a recent decision upholding the mail fraud statute against a vagueness challenge, the Second Circuit, after admitting that the statute's meaning was not plain enough on its face to satisfy the constitutional standard, found the "well-settled meaning of scheme or artifice to deprive another of the intangible right of honest services"[68] to be

> a scheme or artifice to use the mails or wires to enable an officer or employee of a private entity (or a person in a relationship that gives rise to a duty of loyalty comparable to that owed by employees to employers) purporting to act for and in the interests of his or her employer (or of the other person to whom the duty of loyalty is owed) secretly to act in his or her or the defendant's own interests instead, accompanied by a material misrepresentation made or omission of information disclosed to the employer or other person.[69]

But, as the dissent pointed out, this standard "in effect criminalizes all material acts of dishonesty by employees or by persons who owe analogous duties,"[70] and would thus allow the criminal punishment

> of any of the following conduct: a regulated company that employs a political spouse; an employee who violates an employee code of conduct; a lawyer who provides sky-box tickets to a client's general counsel; a trustee who makes a self-dealing investment that pays off; or an officeholder who has made a decision in order to please a constituent or contributor, or to promote re-election, rather than for the public good (as some prosecutor may see the public good).[71]

Because "[e]very salaried employee can be said to work for her own interest while purporting to act in the interests of the employer,"[72] and because "the majority opinion effectively makes 'dishonesty by an employee, standing alone, a crime,'"[73] the "well-settled meaning" of the mail fraud statute appears to place very little limitation on the exercise of prosecutorial discretion. And because the statute can apparently apply to virtually any form of dishonest or deceptive behavior, it gives the public very little notice of what the criminal law demands of them beyond a general injunction to render honest services.

Secondly, the new regulatory offenses mitigated the prosecutor's burden of proving *mens rea*. Intent is typically the most difficult element for a prosecutor to establish. This is especially true in the corporate environment with its diffuse responsibility and is further magnified in cases dealing with complex regulatory requirements in which proving willful conduct requires the prosecutor to establish that the defendant knew that he or she was violating the law.[74] Public welfare offenses eliminate this burden entirely. Similarly, regulatory offenses that require only ordinary negligence reduce the burden to relative insignificance, because by permitting convictions to be based on the violation of an objective, reasonable person standard, these offenses eliminate the need for the prosecutor to introduce any evidence of what was actually in the defendant's mind.

Dispensing with the need to prove intent is a great boon to federal prosecutors in that it converts the task of applying criminal sanctions to regulatory violations from one that is virtually impossible to one that is merely difficult. But once again, this boon does not come without cost. Because "the state of mind that accompanies one's act is entirely within the individual's control,"[75] requiring the government to prove intent "substantially increase[s] the individual's power to control his freedom from punishment."[76] Conversely, dispensing with the need to prove intent substantially decreases the extent to which individuals can exercise that power. Thus, the cost of improving prosecutorial efficiency is the concomitant reduction in the assurance individuals can have that they will not inadvertently become enmeshed in the coils of the criminal law.

Finally, the new secondary offenses provide prosecutors with a convenient route around the requirements of the presumption of innocence and proof beyond reasonable doubt. As has already been noted, obtaining a conviction for one of the secondary offenses does not require establishing that the defendant is guilty of any underlying substantive criminal offense.[77] This feature permits prosecutors to use the secondary offenses as vehicles to punish those individuals whom they suspect, but cannot convict, of substantive criminal offenses. Consider, for example, the use prosecutors can make of the money laundering statutes, which typically carry harsher sentences than most substantive white-collar offenses and whose elements are easier to establish. As two federal prosecutors themselves point out,

> [i]n addition to higher sentences in white collar cases, there are other advantages to federal prosecutors in pursuing money laundering charges against defendants, including: . . . the ability to prosecute a wrongdoer when there is either insufficient evidence of the underlying criminal conduct or insufficient evidence connecting the wrongdoer to the underlying criminal conduct. . . . [T]he money laundering statutes allow prosecutors to prosecute wrongdoers who very probably were involved in the underlying crime without enough evidence of this involvement to prosecute it directly. Thus evidence of the underlying crime which may be insufficient to prove all the elements of the underlying crime may still be enough to show that a specified unlawful activity occurred— leading to a money laundering conviction even if the defendant is acquitted of the underlying crime.[78]

Indeed, in *United States v. Jackson*,[79] the defendant's conviction on money laundering charges was upheld despite the fact that he was acquitted on the underlying substantive charge of drug trafficking.

The false statements and obstruction of justice statutes can similarly be used to circumvent the need to prove every element of a substantive criminal offense beyond reasonable doubt. It is entirely possible that certain employees of Arthur Andersen did engage in fraudulent activities in connection with the auditing of Enron's books and, hence, that Arthur Andersen itself was guilty of a substantive offense. Bringing such a case, however, would be an arduous and expensive task. Prosecutors would have to invest the resources necessary to subpoena and review an extensive amount of documentation, interview potentially dozens of Andersen and Enron employees who might invoke their privilege against self-incrimination, unravel a complex scheme of deception disguised to look like legally proper behavior, and establish either that at least one employee was acting intentionally in the scope of his or her employment, or that the partnership had sufficient collective knowledge to be aware that fraud was taking place.

Convicting Arthur Andersen of obstruction of justice, however, required the government to prove only that at least one person in the company attempted to corruptly persuade others to alter or destroy a document or documents that might be sought in connection with an investigation by a federal agency.[80] Similarly, it is considerably easier to obtain an obstruction of justice conviction against former prominent high-tech investment banker Frank Quattrone for forwarding a single e-mail than it is to develop the evidence necessary to prove beyond reasonable doubt that he was a knowing participant in a fraudulent scheme to charge higher than usual commissions to hedge funds in return for favorable allocations of initial public offerings. Finally, in the Martha Stewart case, the government was unable to establish the elements of insider trading, not for evidentiary reasons, but because one of the necessary elements of the offense, that Stewart be an insider or have misappropriated confidential information, was missing. The prosecution was nevertheless able to circumvent the impossibility of meeting its burden of proof on the underlying substantive offense by charging and convicting Stewart of making false statements to federal investigators and obstructing an agency investigation.

6. The Solutions—The Organizational Sentencing Guidelines

The advent of corporate criminal responsibility and the legislative creation of new white-collar offenses considerably eased the burden that the liberal aspects of traditional criminal law imposed upon federal prosecutors. Nevertheless, large corporations typically have extensive resources at their disposal with which to put on a defense, and they can use those resources to hire the most experienced and sophisticated members of the white-collar criminal defense bar. Thus, to the extent that they are willing to defend themselves against criminal charges, corporations still constitute a formidable adversary for federal prosecutors. Anything that would make corporations less likely to mount such a defense would be a welcome addition to the prosecutors' arsenal. Just such an addition arrived in 1991 in the form of Chapter 8 of the U.S. Sentencing Commission's *Federal Sentencing Guidelines Manual, the Organizational Sentencing Guidelines.*[1]

The Organizational Sentencing Guidelines are designed to govern the sentencing of corporate entities convicted of violating federal law. Because such entities cannot be imprisoned, the guidelines consist of a schedule of fines to be levied against corporate violators that are determined on the basis of the offense committed and the organization's corporate character as captured by a "culpability score." Although the guidelines are complex, the aspects that are relevant to our present concerns are reasonably straightforward.

When an organization is convicted of a federal offense, the fine it must pay is determined by multiplying a base fine by an amount derived from the organization's culpability score.[2] The base fine is the greatest of: (1) the amount assigned to the offense that the organization has committed by an offense-level fine table; (2) the pecuniary gain to the organization from the offense; or (3) the pecuniary loss from the offense knowingly caused by the organization.[3] The offense-level fine table assigns fines ranging from $5,000 to $72,500,000 for the various federal offenses in proportion to their severity.[4] The resulting base fine "is intended to reflect the intrinsic seriousness of the underlying offense for which the organization bears vicarious liability."[5]

The organization's culpability score consists of a number from 0 to 10 that is determined by assigning every organization a starting point of 5, which is then adjusted upward or downward on the basis of seven enumerated mitigating or aggravating factors.[6] Three of those factors are of particular relevance to our present consideration. The first is the aggravating factor for obstructing justice, which adds three points to the organization's score if the organization obstructed, attempted to obstruct, or knowingly failed to take reasonable steps to prevent the obstruction of justice.[7] The second is the mitigating factor for having an effective compliance program, which deducts three points if the offense occurred despite an effective program to prevent and detect violations of law.[8] And the third is the mitigating factor for cooperation, which deducts five points

> [i]f the organization (A) prior to an imminent threat of disclosure or government investigation; and (B) within a reasonably prompt time after becoming aware of the offense, reported the offense to appropriate governmental authorities, fully cooperated in the investigation, and clearly demonstrated recognition and affirmative acceptance of responsibility for its criminal conduct. . . .[9]

The culpability score that results from this calculation is designed to encapsulate "the organization's institutional response to the offense, both before and after its commission."[10]

The organization's culpability score is associated with minimum and maximum multipliers whose values range from .05 to 4.00.[11] For example, a culpability score of 0 is assigned a minimum multiplier of 0.05 and a maximum multiplier of 0.20, while a culpability score of 10 is assigned a minimum multiplier of 2.00 and a maximum multiplier of 4.00.[12] The base fine is then multiplied by both the minimum and the maximum multiplier to determine the guideline's fine range from which the judge must assign the organization's fine.[13]

A moment's reflection reveals the overwhelming importance of the organization's culpability score, which can reduce the organization's fine by 95 percent or increase it by 400 percent. This feature creates an almost irresistible incentive for organizations to achieve the lowest possible score. As a result, organizations have the strongest possible reasons for seeking to avoid the three-point increase for obstructing justice and to receive the three- and five-point reductions for having an effective compliance program and for cooperation. Consider what achieving this goal requires.

To avoid the enhancement to its culpability score for obstruction of justice, the organization must not only not obstruct or attempt to obstruct a federal investigation, it must also not knowingly fail to take reasonable steps to prevent such obstruction. In other words, to avoid the enhancement, the organization must take all reasonable steps to ensure that none of its employees take actions that can constitute obstruction. But as the Andersen and Quattrone cases demonstrate, obstruction of justice can consist of recommending that someone alter, destroy, or conceal anything that may be relevant to a federal investigation.[14] It may also consist of persuading someone not to speak to federal investigators[15] or to assert his or her Fifth Amendment rights.[16] Thus, to avoid the enhancement for obstruction, organizations must make every reasonable effort both to preserve anything that can be used as evidence against it and to ensure that no one is wrongfully discouraged from providing such evidence to the government. As a result, an organization that permitted its corporate counsel to advise employees not to make statements to federal investigators, or to suggest that they assert their Fifth Amendment rights to protect the organization rather than themselves could, if convicted, receive a greater fine for doing so. That possibility can significantly raise the risk associated with electing to mount a vigorous defense to a criminal charge.

To receive the reduction to its culpability score for having an effective compliance program, the organization must "exercise due diligence to prevent and detect criminal conduct."[17] Such due diligence requires that the organization undertake not only the criminal investigative function—that it engage in "monitoring and auditing [the behavior of its employees] to detect criminal conduct" and maintain a system "whereby the organization's employees and agents may report or seek guidance regarding potential or actual criminal conduct without fear of retribution"[18]—but to some extent the punitive function as well—that it impose "appropriate disciplinary measures for engaging in criminal conduct."[19] In essence, for an organization convicted of a federal offense to receive a reduced fine for having an effective compliance program, it must have a program designed to generate precisely the evidence of criminal wrongdoing on the part of its employees that the government can use to convict the organization itself. Whether or not such activity is a reasonable indication of good corporate character, as the Organizational Guidelines assumes, it is not necessarily consistent with an organization's efforts to vigorously defend itself against criminal charges.

Finally, to receive the all-important five-point reduction for cooperation, the organization must voluntarily disclose its wrongful conduct in a timely manner, fully cooperate in the government's investigation of that behavior, and clearly accept responsibility for its criminal conduct.[20] For the disclosure to be timely, it must be made before an imminent threat of disclosure or government investigation and within a reasonably prompt time after the organization becomes aware of the offense.[21] This requirement essentially means "as soon as possible" because the disclosure is considered untimely once a government investigation commences, whether the organization is aware of that investigation or not.[22] Full cooperation requires the organization to cooperate from the inception of the government investigation and to disclose "all pertinent information known by the organization,"[23] which should include information that "is sufficient for law enforcement personnel to identify the nature and extent of the offense and the individual(s) responsible for the criminal conduct."[24] Acceptance of responsibility essentially requires an organization to plead guilty to the offense charged *without putting on a defense*. The reasoning is that, although the

> [e]ntry of a plea of guilty prior to the commencement of trial combined with truthful admission of involvement in the offense and related conduct ordinarily will constitute significant evidence of affirmative acceptance of responsibility under subsection (g), . . . [t]his adjustment is not intended to apply to an organization that puts the government to its burden of proof at trial by denying the essential factual elements of guilt. . . .[25]

Needless to say, this provision creates a strong disincentive for an organization to mount a defense to federal charges. Indeed, "under the Guidelines, the price a defendant pays for exercising its constitutional right to trial is the preclusion of the possibility of having its culpability score reduced . . . under Section 8C2.5(g)."[26]

Significantly, the determination of whether an organization has cooperated sufficiently to be eligible for the five-point reduction in its culpability score rests with the prosecutors. Because courts will not award the reduction without a recommendation from the prosecutor, cooperation is, for all intents and purposes, what prosecutors say it is.[27] And, pursuant to a 2003 memorandum issued by Deputy Attorney General Larry D. Thompson containing the Justice Department's policy on cooperation (hereinafter the Thompson Memorandum),[28] prosecutors frequently say that it amounts to a corporation's willingness to waive attorney-client privilege, to refrain from paying its employees' legal fees, and to refuse to enter into joint defense agreements with its employees.[29]

With regard to the waiver of attorney-client privilege, the Thompson Memorandum states that

> [o]ne factor the prosecutor may weigh in assessing the adequacy of a corporation's cooperation is the completeness of its disclosure including, if necessary, a waiver of the attorney-client and work product protections, both with respect to its internal investigation and with respect to communications between specific officers, directors and employees and counsel. Such waivers permit the government to obtain statements of possible witnesses, subjects, and targets, without having to negotiate individual cooperation or immunity agreements. . . . [P]rosecutors should consider the willingness of a corporation to waive such protection when necessary to provide timely and complete information as one factor in evaluating the corporation's cooperation.[30]

In accordance with this policy, federal prosecutors now routinely require corporations to waive attorney-client and work product privileges at the outset of an investigation in order to be regarded as fully cooperating.[31] As the Thompson Memorandum makes clear in stating that "[s]uch waivers permit the government to obtain statements of possible witnesses, subjects, and targets, without having to negotiate individual cooperation or immunity agreements,"[32] "there is no pretense that the values underlying these privileges are to be sacrificed for any reason other than to make the prosecution's job easier."[33] Accordingly, "[t]he Justice Department does not merely seek disclosure of contemporaneous legal advice concerning the underlying conduct at issue in an investigation. It also asks for the 'factual internal investigation,' presumably because access to such attorney work product is an easy way to obtain evidence that the government formerly had to generate on its own."[34] Because "[t]he prosecutor can influence the severity of the sentence . . . by recommending the deduction of cooperation points from the Guidelines calculation, . . . federal prosecutors can demand that companies disclose privileged information at the outset of an investigation, and the client is often left with no rational choice but to accede."[35]

With regard to the payment of employees' attorney's fees and entering into joint defense agreements with employees, the Thompson Memorandum states that

> [a]nother factor to be weighed by the prosecutor is whether the corporation appears to be protecting its culpable employees and agents. Thus, while cases will differ depending on the circumstances, a corporation's promise of support to culpable employees and agents, either through the advancing of attorneys fees, through retaining the employees without sanction for their misconduct, or through providing information to the employees about the government's investigation pursuant to a joint defense agreement, may be considered by the prosecutor in weighing the extent and value of a corporation's cooperation.[36]

Thus, even an organization that waives attorney-client privilege may still be denied the reduction for cooperating if it advances the legal fees of an employee whom the government regards as guilty,[37] fails to fire such an employee, or agrees to cooperate with such an employee in preparing his or her defense. "Prosecutors have seized upon the new guidelines language and the Thompson Memorandum's discussion of privilege waiver and now regularly take the position that the only way for a company to avoid indictment is to cooperate, which requires waiving the privilege *and not assisting or protecting employees who are targets*."[38] The effect of these incentives is illustrated by the case of the accounting firm of KPMG, which is under investigation for tax shelters that it sold to its clients.[39] KPMG

> is cooperating with the government and refusing to assist partners and employees whom the government deems as uncooperative. KPMG refused to pay the legal fees of its partners and employees unless they agreed to cooperate with the prosecutors, refused to enter joint defense agreements

> with its partners, agreed to tell prosecutors which documents
> the employees and partners are requesting, and fired or
> threatened to fire those employees whom the government
> indicates are not cooperating.[40]

As considerations such as these make apparent, the Organizational
Sentencing Guidelines provide prosecutors with a powerful tool for
circumventing the inherent liberalism of the criminal law. To begin
with, the guidelines constitute an extraordinarily effective means of
reducing the strain on the prosecutorial resources that result from
having to overcome the presumption of innocence. There is no need
to bear the expense required to establish every element of an offense
beyond reasonable doubt if the defendant pleads guilty. By increasing the potential cost of taking a case to trial, the guidelines discourage organizations from putting on a defense at all. The increased
level of fines that an organization can receive by going to trial and
losing rather than by pleading guilty and cooperating can be so
massive (the difference between multiplying the base fine by .05
and by 4) that it will usually be economically irrational for the
organization to maintain its innocence. Indeed, the guidelines can
have such a profound effect on the organization's bottom line that
John Coffee of the Columbia Law School has declared that "[f]or a
general counsel to ignore these guidelines is professional malprac-
tice."[41] Thus, to the extent that the guidelines effectively incentivize
organizations to plead guilty, federal prosecutors are relieved of the
burden of overcoming the presumption of innocence.

But the guidelines do much more than merely discourage organizations from mounting a defense to charges brought against it as a
corporate entity. To a great extent, they turn organizations into an
auxiliary in the prosecution of its employees as individuals. The
"stick" of the increase in culpability score for obstruction of justice
and the "carrots" of the reductions for compliance programs and
cooperation essentially present organizations with a tripartite injunction to (1) do nothing that would help its employees defend themselves against criminal charges or discourage them from cooperating
with the government, (2) perform a thorough criminal investigation
of its employees, and (3) turn the results of this investigation over
to the government. Unsurprisingly, given the size of the incentives
involved, business organizations frequently comply with the
injunction.

> More so than ever before, corporations faced with significant criminal investigations are cooperating with the government by collecting and analyzing documents relating to the suspected criminal activity, interviewing employees, conducting costly and time-consuming internal investigations and forensic audits, and turning over the results of this work to the government. . . . In a clear sign that a cooperating company becomes an arm of the government, a few months ago federal prosecutors in the Eastern District of New York charged corporate executives of Computer Associates International Inc. with obstruction of justice for false statements they made to the company's outside counsel during an internal investigation; they pleaded guilty.[42]

Thus, the guidelines allow prosecutors to pass the costs of criminal investigations along to private businesses. In effect, they convert part of the expense of establishing the guilt of individual white-collar criminal defendants from a charge on the federal budget into a cost of doing business in the United States. This is a particularly effective way of avoiding the presumption of innocence's injunction that "the government not only . . . establish its case, but [do] so by its own resources."[43]

It should not be surprising that the Organizational Guidelines function in that way. As previously discussed, regardless of the size of the Justice Department's budget, the department could not effectively enforce the laws against white-collar crime if it was required to prove every offense beyond reasonable doubt with its own resources.[44] The number of businesses in the United States is simply too great and the opportunities for dishonest conduct and regulatory violation too vast for any centralized agency to be able to effectively police the business environment. The nature of the conduct that is criminalized by the white-collar offenses implies that effective enforcement requires that businesses be made to police themselves. The presumption of innocence of the traditional criminal law is thus incompatible with the effective enforcement of white-collar criminal law. Hence, the internal logic of white-collar criminal law itself leads to the incentives that are built into the guidelines. The guidelines contain such incentives because one of their essential functions is to conscript businesses into the war on white-collar crime.[45]

A second important effect of the Organizational Guidelines is that they enable prosecutors to circumvent the organization's attorney-client privilege. As discussed previously, organizations have no Fifth Amendment privilege against self-incrimination.[46] Therefore, the organization's attorney-client privilege is the only impediment to a prosecutor obtaining all potentially incriminating evidence in the possession of a corporate defendant. By empowering prosecutors to deny organizations the five-point reduction in their culpability score for cooperation unless they waive attorney-client privilege,[47] the guidelines effectively emasculate the privilege by making it too costly to assert. This power ultimately gives prosecutors open access to all corporate records for the purpose of building a case against both the organization and its employees.

The advantage of such access for prosecutors is not so much that it provides them with otherwise unobtainable information, but that it greatly reduces the cost of developing obtainable information on their own. The attorney-client privilege protects only communications made to and by the organization's counsel in anticipation of litigation.[48] Hence, it does not allow an organization to prevent the prosecution from obtaining any factual evidence of criminal activity. As the Supreme Court has pointed out, "[a]pplication of the attorney-client privilege to communications . . . puts the adversary in no worse position than if the communications had never taken place. The privilege only protects disclosure of communications; it does not protect disclosure of the underlying facts by those who communicated with the attorney."[49] Thus, "[t]he client cannot be compelled to answer the question, 'What did you say or write to the attorney?' but may not refuse to disclose any relevant fact within his knowledge merely because he incorporated a statement of such fact into his communication to his attorney."[50] Accordingly, prosecutors are free to question any and all corporate employees in an attempt to develop evidence of criminal activity themselves. This undertaking, however, can be expensive both in man-hours and because employees tend to be less forthcoming with police agents than they are with corporate counsel. Furthermore, unlike organizations, individuals do possess a Fifth Amendment right against self-incrimination, which they may assert in order to refrain from supplying information to the government. Thus, getting access to the internal investigations performed by corporate counsel allows prosecutors both to avoid the expense of performing the investigation themselves and to obtain information that would otherwise be barred by individuals' Fifth Amendment rights. By inducing organizations to waive their attorney-client privileges, the guidelines allow prosecutors to kill two liberal birds with one stone: circumventing not only the corporate common law privilege but also the individual constitutional one.

Finally, the Organizational Guidelines help prosecutors avoid having to overcome the presumption of innocence in their cases against individuals as well. By requiring organizations not only to refrain from helping their employees prepare a defense, but to affirmatively aid the government in making its case against them in order to get the culpability score reduction for cooperation, the guidelines greatly increase both the cost and the risk that individual employees face in electing to go to trial. Given that white-collar criminal defense costs can frequently run in the hundreds of thousands of dollars,[51] the refusal to advance employees' legal fees can bring intense pressure on individual employees to plead guilty. That financial pressure is exacerbated by the fact that, by defending themselves, the employees are refusing to cooperate with the government, and thus, under the Thompson Memorandum, the organization must fire them in order to be assured that it will be regarded as cooperating.[52] Adding to the pressure is the increased risk of conviction that arises from the organization not only turning over all incriminating evidence to the government but also informing the government of any request for documents or information that the employees may make in preparing their defense. Under those circumstances, a significant number of individual targets of federal investigations will elect to forgo their day in court and plead guilty, which, of course, entirely relieves prosecutors of the burden of establishing guilt beyond reasonable doubt.

It is worth noting that the recent United States Supreme Court decision in *United States v. Booker*, rendering the Federal Sentencing Guidelines advisory rather than mandatory, works no significant change in this situation because the guidelines still serve as the basic framework for determining an organization's fine. Although *Booker* permits judges to depart from the guideline's sentencing range when circumstances warrant, the decision does not affect the ordinary case. Judges will still calculate and be guided by an organization's culpability score, which means the incentives created by the enhancement for obstruction of justice and the reductions for having an effective compliance program and for cooperation will still be in effect. Furthermore, the decisions have no effect at all on the Thompson Memorandum, so the guidelines' incentives for cooperation will still be operative as a means of avoiding indictment—something that is more important to organizations than merely reducing their fines upon conviction. Finally, organizations will be aware that should they be indicted, their ability to receive the five-point culpability score reduction for cooperation still depends on their receiving a recommendation to that effect from the prosecutor, whose standards for cooperation are likewise governed by the Thompson Memorandum. Hence, *Booker* does not undermine any of the arguments advanced in this chapter.

PART II

THE EFFECT OF THE FEDERAL CAMPAIGN
AGAINST WHITE-COLLAR CRIME

7. Five Ethical Dilemmas

The traditional criminal law may be an adequate mechanism for combating violent crime or actions that directly harm or violate the rights of others. Its inherent liberal features, however, make it a poor tool for extending the kind of social control necessary to suppress general dishonest or deceptive behavior and the violation of *malum prohibitum* regulations. By nevertheless criminalizing such conduct, the federal government created a body of law that it could not effectively enforce within the confines of the traditional criminal law. Hence, the internal logic of the federal campaign against white-collar crime required significant alterations to both the substance and the procedures of the criminal law that would eliminate, or permit the circumvention of, several of its liberal safeguards. Those alterations arrived via the recognition of the concept of corporate criminal responsibility; the creation of broad new substantive, regulatory, and secondary offenses; and the adoption of the Organizational Sentencing Guidelines. The principal effect of the first and third of these innovations was to effectively deputize America's business organizations as auxiliary law enforcement agents, while the principal effect of the second was to vastly expand the range of activities within the ambit of the criminal sanction.

These alterations to the workings of the criminal law significantly changed the environment within which corporate officers make managerial decisions. Most significantly, they changed the legal rewards and punishments associated with the way organizations treat their employees. If ethics were coextensive with obedience to law, this change would not constitute a problem. Acting in accordance with the law and its incentives would be equivalent to acting ethically, and organizations need have no qualms about treating their employees in whatever way the law demanded. But ethics is not coextensive with legality, and responding to legal incentives does not guarantee that an organization is acting ethically, as the Jim Crow legislation that mandated racial segregation makes abundantly clear. Therefore, to the extent that white-collar criminal law induces organizations to treat their employees improperly or to violate any other ethical obligation, it can create difficult and poignant ethical dilemmas for the organizations' managers.

There is currently a wide range of opinions regarding the nature and extent of businesspersons' ethical obligations. On one end of the ideological spectrum is the so-called stockholder theory,[1] which views corporate officers as agents of the organization's owners (the stockholders) who have a fiduciary obligation to pursue their principals' interests, usually characterized as the maximization of profits, in preference to the interests of all other parties. At the other end of the spectrum are the stakeholder and social contract theories, which view corporate officers as having ethical obligations to not merely the organization's owners, but, in the case of the stakeholder theory, to all parties whose interests are significantly affected by the organization's activities, such as employees, customers, suppliers, and the local community;[2] or, in the case of the social contract theory, to society as a whole.[3]

But all of these theories share two common features—they recognize that businesspeople retain all the ordinary ethical obligations that they possess as human beings[4] and they instruct businesspeople to fulfill their ethical obligations within the law. Thus, to the extent the law requires businesspeople to act in ways that would violate either their personal ethical obligations or those additional obligations that arise from their status as corporate officers, a businessperson's legal and ethical obligations are in conflict. The question then becomes which obligation should predominate. Currently, this question arises in at least five areas of managerial decisionmaking—those concerning the organization's efforts to (1) realize organizational justice, (2) properly respect employees' privacy, (3) maintain needed confidentiality, (4) engender trust within the organization, and (5) engage in ethical self-assessment.

8. Organizational Justice

Questions of justice are not limited to the realm of the law. Although justice may be the cardinal virtue of a legal system, legal justice is not all of justice. Justice is the general virtue that requires the fair treatment of individuals in all interpersonal relationships.[1] Because business organizations consist of networks of interpersonal relationships, questions of justice necessarily arise in the context of organizations as well. Organizations have an ethical obligation to treat their employees justly. But precisely what does this obligation entail?

That question may be asked from both a deontological and a consequentialist perspective. From a deontological perspective, the question would be whether justice demands that organizations treat their employees in certain ways as a matter of principle, regardless of the consequences. In the context of this book, this perspective amounts to the question of what principles govern the treatment of employees who are suspected of criminal wrongdoing by federal authorities. At least three principles are implicated—reciprocity, the presumption of innocence, and due process.

Reciprocity refers to an individual's obligation to honor a commitment to a mutually beneficial relationship when the other party has met his or her commitment to that individual. Business organizations expect their employees to exhibit loyalty to the organization and to advance the organization's interests in preference to those of competitors or outside groups.[2] The principle of reciprocity requires that, to the extent that employees act in accordance with this duty of loyalty, the organization exhibit a similar loyalty to its employees by giving their interests preference over those of outside parties.[3] The presumption of innocence refers to the more general version of the ethical principle that operates within the criminal law. Because of employees' limited resources and dependence on the employer, and because it is so difficult to prove a negative, justice requires that organizations not assume that their employees have behaved improperly in the absence of adequate evidence. The presumption of innocence may also be seen as derivative of the principle of reciprocity in the sense that it constitutes a specific instance of the loyalty that an organization owes to its employees in return for its employees' loyalty to the organization. Finally, due process refers to the requirement that one be judged by fair processes, which include an opportunity to speak in one's own defense. Like the presumption of innocence, due process may be seen as either a general requirement of justice or as an obligation derived from the principle of reciprocity.

If justice truly demands that organizations act in accordance with the principles of reciprocity, the presumption of innocence, and due process, then a business manager's legal and ethical obligations will come into conflict. We have seen that the concept of corporate criminal responsibility and the requirements of the Organizational Sentencing Guidelines place the organization and its employees in an adversarial relationship. Because the organization is strictly liable for the actions that its employees perform within the scope of their employment, the only way for the organization to reduce its exposure to financial penalties is to cooperate with the government in its investigation of the organization's employees. But as previously noted, under the guidelines, cooperation requires the organization to essentially become part of the prosecutorial team.[4] And this consequence, in turn, requires the organization to violate all three principles of organizational justice.

When the question arises of whether an organization's employees are engaged in criminal wrongdoing, there are only three epistemological possibilities—the organization may know that the employee is guilty, it may know that the employee is innocent, or it may not know whether the employee is guilty or innocent. If the organization knows that the employee is guilty, there may be no problem. In such a case, cooperating with the prosecution would breach neither the principle of reciprocity nor the presumption of innocence because, by breaking the law, the employee breached his or her duty of loyalty to the organization and hence is entitled to none in return, and because the organization has, by hypothesis, adequate evidence of guilt. On the other hand, even in this case, there may be a due process problem because even the guilty are entitled to a fair hearing before being subject to sanction, and the guidelines' timeliness requirement for cooperation can require an organization to take action against an employee without delay.[5]

If the organization knows the employee is innocent, however, the guidelines place it in an impossible situation. To gain the five-point reduction in its culpability score for cooperation, the organization must help the government try to convict an innocent person. The organization must breach reciprocity by eschewing aid to a loyal employee, act in contravention of the presumption of innocence by taking action against the employee despite the lack of evidence of wrongdoing, and violate due process by either denying the employee a fair hearing or acting in derogation of what such a hearing would establish. Yet, if the organization's managers do not act in this way, they expose the organization to criminal indictment and potentially massive financial penalties.

The same holds true in those cases in which the organization does not know whether the employee is guilty or innocent—a situation in which organizations will frequently find themselves because of the indistinct border between lawful and criminal conduct associated with broadly defined crimes such as the federal fraud offenses.[6] This is precisely the situation in which the principles of organizational justice are most pertinent because they instruct organizations to give employees the benefit of the doubt. In this situation, reciprocity, the presumption of innocence, and due process may require organizations to provide their employees with legal advice, help them to defray the cost of defending themselves, and retain them in their positions until their guilt or innocence is established. Yet, this is precisely the type of behavior that the guidelines discourage.

A similar result obtains if one views questions of justice from a consequentialist (result-oriented) perspective. Over the past several decades, a great deal of academic and managerial attention has been devoted to the internal dynamics of organizations.[7] Scholars engaged in such "organizational behavior" research study how individuals respond to incentives in organizations in an effort to build better interpersonal relationships that allow organizations to achieve their objectives more effectively. One aspect of such study concerns how the fairness with which employees are treated and perceive themselves as being treated affects both the employees' and the organization's performance. The research demonstrates that organizations that are committed to providing procedural justice[8] to their employees have employees who are more satisfied with their jobs and

63

exhibit higher levels of commitment to the organization's goals.[9] In other words, organizations whose employees view themselves as being treated fairly tend to perform better than those whose employees do not.[10] Thus, regardless of whether one adheres to the stakeholder or social contract theories that posit an independent obligation to employees,[11] or to the stockholder theory that instructs managers to create the most efficient organization,[12] managers have, all other things being equal, an ethical obligation to ensure the just treatment of the organization's employees. However, since the Organizational Sentencing Guidelines took effect, all other things are not equal. Now, maintaining corporate policies of procedural justice with regard to employees under federal investigation can subject the organization to indictment or a greatly increased fine. Under these circumstances, it is no longer clear that preserving organizational justice is in the organization's best interest.

Managers then, are faced with conflicting legal and ethical obligations that require them to make extremely difficult decisions. If the law demands cooperation, does that make it ethical to help the government prosecute employees who are or might be innocent or to deny organizational due process to such employees? On the other hand, is it ethical to put the stockholders' money and the well-being of the organization's other stakeholders at risk merely to give a fair hearing to those employees who may well have broken the law and put the organization in jeopardy?

Think back to the first vignette at the beginning of this book. If you were the CEO of Marsha Tudor Styles and sincerely believed Tudor to be innocent of the offenses with which she is charged, would you act on this belief? Should you? Does MTS owe any loyalty to Tudor? If so, how much? Enough to put the company at risk by standing by her until her guilt is established? The combination of corporate criminal responsibility, which holds organizations strictly liable for the offenses of its employees, and the Organizational Sentencing Guidelines, which effectively punish organizations for putting on a (losing) defense, drives a financial wedge between the interests of the organization and its employees. Thus, the contemporary law of white-collar crime literally confronts corporate managers with an age-old ethical dilemma: what price loyalty?

9. Privacy

Like justice, privacy has both a legal and an ethical dimension. The constitutional right to privacy protects individuals against state and federal government interference with certain intimate decisions and conduct, and the common law right to privacy protects them against certain invasions of their private space and unwanted revelations of private facts by their fellow citizens. But these legal protections do not necessarily exhaust the amount of privacy that individuals are morally entitled to enjoy. The moral right to privacy refers to a wider realm of protection against intrusion into one's personal affairs, the public dissemination of one's secrets, and the type of constant supervision and monitoring associated with Orwell's *1984*.[1] Thus, ethically speaking, "[t]he concept of privacy limits the amount and effectiveness of social control over an individual. . . . Privacy protects the individual by limiting scrutiny by others and the control some of them have over our lives."[2]

Employees of private business organizations have little legal protection against their employer's invasion of their privacy in the workplace.[3] Because constitutional provisions do not apply to private actions, employers legally can, and sometimes do, subject their employees to intense monitoring.[4] Ethical requirements to respect individuals' privacy do apply to the workplace, however, and limit the extent to which business organizations may legitimately spy on their employees. From the stakeholder and social contract perspectives, employees' rights to privacy in the workplace flow either from the organization's obligation to respect the dignity of their stakeholder groups, which include employees,[5] or from an implicit term in the social contract between society and business organizations.[6] Furthermore, even from the stockholder perspective, organizations have an ethical obligation to respect employees' privacy because, like the maintenance of organizational justice, doing so produces a workforce that performs better and is more committed to the organization's success.[7]

By entering into the employment relationship, employees waive their right to privacy to a certain degree. Employers are entitled to job-related information about their employees—information that is necessary to ensure that employees can adequately perform their jobs in an appropriate manner.[8] Employers are also entitled to monitor their employees' behavior to the extent necessary to ensure that they do so perform.[9] But employers are not ethically entitled to pry into employees' personal lives or to monitor employees' behavior for other purposes, even though acquiring such information or engaging in such action may improve overall corporate performance. The law of white-collar crime, however, virtually requires business organizations to exceed these ethical constraints.

Because the standard for corporate criminal responsibility makes organizations strictly liable for the offenses of their employees, organizations can avoid criminal liability only by preventing their employees from violating the law. This pressure is reinforced by the Organizational Sentencing Guidelines, which provide a three-point reduction in an organization's culpability score for maintaining an effective program designed to prevent and detect criminal conduct by its employees.[10] But an organization can prevent its employees from violating the law only by gathering sufficient information about them to allow the organization to determine who is likely to violate the law and by intensely monitoring the actions that its employees take within the scope of their employment. Indeed, this behavior is precisely what the guidelines require. An effective compliance program requires organizations to "use reasonable efforts not to include within the substantial authority personnel of the organization any individual whom the organization knew, *or should have known through the exercise of due diligence*, has engaged in illegal activities or other conduct inconsistent with an effective compliance and ethics program,"[11] and to "take reasonable steps to ensure that the organization's compliance and ethics program is followed, including *monitoring and auditing to detect criminal conduct*."[12] Therefore, the law creates incentives for organizations to violate their employees' privacy in ways that conflict with the organizations' ethical obligations not to do so.

Once again, corporate managers are confronted with difficult ethical choices. Do legal obligations to act as deputy law enforcement agents trump their ethical obligations to respect their employees' dignity? If not, how much risk of criminal liability or increased criminal penalties are managers required to run? To what extent is it ethical to jeopardize the stockholders' and other stakeholders' material interests in order to preserve the intangible interests of the organization's employees? Putting yourself again in the place of the hypothetical CEO of MTS, recall that cooperation with the government requires the organization to review and turn over to the prosecution the records of all of Tudor's appointments, phone calls, e-mail correspondence, and personal revelations made in confidence to the organization's corporate counsel. How sure are you that this is the ethically correct thing to do?

10. Confidentiality

There is good reason to believe that organizations are ethically obligated to maintain the confidentiality of certain internal communications. Like organizational justice and privacy, this obligation derives from both principled and practical considerations. The principle involved is the basic ethical obligation to keep one's word. If one party reveals information to a second only because the latter promises to keep the information confidential, the promise ethically binds the second party to do so. This is equally true when the second party is an organization that is promising confidentiality to an employee or other stakeholder. To obtain information under a promise of confidentiality and then disclose it under circumstances not agreed to by the confiding party is essentially to obtain the information by means of a false promise that the confiding party relied on in revealing the information. Such action is ethically indistinguishable from fraud.

On the practical level, confidentiality is necessary to facilitate the flow of information through the organization. Employees (and outsiders) will often be unwilling to reveal information when they believe they will suffer adverse consequences if it becomes known they have done so. This reluctance is especially true with regard to information indicating that they, their colleagues, or their superiors are involved in unethical or illegal behavior. Thus, only by promising confidentiality can organizations guarantee that their management will receive the information necessary for them to run not only efficiently, but ethically and legally as well.

Like the obligations to maintain organizational justice and respect employee privacy, the obligation to preserve promised confidentiality is recognized by all normative approaches to business ethics. From the stakeholder perspective, the obligation to preserve confidentiality is an aspect of the duty to avoid deceptive and fraudulent dealing that is implicit in the requirement to treat all stakeholders in accordance with the Kantian principle of respect for persons.[1]

From the social contract perspective, the obligation is an explicit requirement of the justice term of the contract, or in more contemporary terminology, a hypernorm, which is binding on all business organizations.[2] Finally, from the stockholder perspective, the obligation is both explicitly recognized by the theory's fundamental directive to maximize profits or otherwise carry out the stockholder's instructions without engaging in fraud or deception,[3] and implicitly found in the fact that preserving confidentiality increases business organizations' efficiency.

Organizations usually promise confidentiality in two ways. First, as a means of gathering sensitive information that otherwise would not be forthcoming, organizations often create lines of communication that circumvent the ordinary corporate chain of command, such as employee hotlines or organizational ombudsmen.[4] To encourage employees to use such alternative lines of communication, organizations typically promise to keep any information transmitted through them confidential. In that way, upper management hopes to receive information from lower-level employees concerning the job performance and ethical behavior of the employees' colleagues and superiors that could not be otherwise obtained. Second, in order to accumulate the information necessary both to defend the organization against civil lawsuits and criminal charges, and to ensure that the organization is complying with the law, organizations encourage their employees to provide information to corporate counsel under the protection of the attorney-client privilege. In other words, organizations promise their employees that if they talk to the organizations' attorneys, what they say will not be revealed to outsiders unless it meets one of the recognized exceptions to the privilege.

Indeed, the Supreme Court has explicitly recognized the importance of an organization's ability to promise the second type of confidentiality.[5] The Court noted that, given the legal standard for corporate criminal responsibility,

> [m]iddle-level—and indeed lower-level—employees can, by actions within the scope of their employment, embroil the corporation in serious legal difficulties, and it is only natural that these employees would have the relevant information needed by corporate counsel if he is adequately to advise the client with respect to such actual or potential difficulties.[6]

Thus, it recognized that the attorney-client privilege is necessary to encourage "the communication of relevant information by employees of the client to attorneys seeking to render legal advice to the client corporation."[7] The Court further recognized that, given the advent of the myriad new substantive, regulatory, and secondary criminal offenses, the privilege was necessary to promote

> the valuable efforts of corporate counsel to ensure their client's compliance with the law. In light of the vast and complicated array of regulatory legislation confronting the modern corporation, corporations, unlike most individuals, "constantly go to lawyers to find out how to obey the law," particularly since compliance with the law in this area is hardly an instinctive matter.[8]

Business organizations' obligation to maintain promised confidentiality is not absolute, of course, but is limited to the amount of confidentiality organizations have it within their power to grant. Employers have never been able to promise employees (or others) complete confidentiality, merely the degree of confidentiality the law allows. Thus, organizations cannot promise to keep revelations confidential in the face of a valid subpoena that does not improperly invade the attorney-client privilege. The most that organizations can, and hence do, is promise their employees is that they will act in good faith to maintain confidentiality to the extent that they are legally permitted to do so.

The incentives created by the law of white-collar crime, however, are at odds with honoring even this limited obligation. As previously noted, organizations' strict liability for the offenses of their employees and the requirements of the Organizational Sentencing Guidelines imply that organizations can avoid indictment or reduce their exposure to financial penalties only by cooperating with government investigations of their employees.[9] But under the guidelines, cooperation requires "the disclosure of all pertinent information known by the organization,"[10] which, in turn, may require the waiver of the attorney-client privilege.[11] Thus, to gain the benefits of cooperation, organizations must disclose to the government not merely all of the information they are legally required to disclose, but all relevant information in their possession. Refusing to do so on the ground that such disclosure would violate a promise of confidentiality could subject an organization to a potentially massive increase in liability.

71

This possibility places corporate managers in an extremely difficult ethical situation. To generate the information necessary to maintain an ethical workplace and to ensure that the organization's employees are complying with the law, management must promise its employees confidentiality. But to avoid subjecting the organization to indictment and large monetary fines, management must not only breach that promise, but must do so before a government investigation has even begun—according to the guidelines, "prior to an imminent threat of disclosure or government investigation."[12]

Furthermore, management cannot avoid the dilemma by making only a conditional promise to keep information confidential unless disclosure is necessary for the organization to cooperate with the government. Such a promise would be patently self-defeating and tantamount to saying that the organization will keep the information confidential unless it is in the organization's interest to disclose it— which is the same as saying the organization will not keep the information confidential at all. This type of promise is obviously valueless—something the Supreme Court recognized in the context of the attorney-client privilege, stating "if the purpose of the attorney-client privilege is to be served, the attorney and client must be able to predict with some degree of certainty whether particular discussions will be protected. An uncertain privilege . . . is little better than no privilege at all."[13] Hence, such a conditional promise will elicit no useful information from the organization's employees and is equivalent to making no promise of confidentiality at all.

But even an organization that decided not to promise any confidentiality for employees' (or others') communications could not escape the dilemma. By refusing on ethical grounds to make a promise that it knows it will have to break, such an organization could decide to conduct its business without the information that such a promise would generate. But in doing so, it would be willingly forgoing one of the most effective means of detecting violations of law by its employees—a decision that would, under the guidelines, cost the organization the three-point reduction in its culpability score that could be gained by having an effective compliance program. As previously noted, one of the requirements for such a program is that the organization "have and publicize a system, which may include mechanisms that allow for anonymity or confidentiality, whereby the organization's employees and agents may report or seek guidance regarding potential or actual criminal conduct without fear of retaliation."[14] But because whistleblowers are usually subject to retaliation if their identity is known, such a reporting system not merely "may," but virtually must, be one that promises confidentiality.[15] Indeed, in the Sarbanes-Oxley Act of 2002, Congress required publicly traded companies to establish procedures for "the *confidential*, anonymous submission by employees of issues or concerns regarding questionable accounting or auditing practices."[16] Thus, even the decision not to make a promise of confidentiality would significantly increase an organization's potential liability. In sum, the law of white-collar crime brings intense pressure to bear on organizations to both make and breach promises of confidentiality.

The conflict thus created presents corporate managers with several difficult ethical decisions. What should they tell employees about the organization's commitment to preserve the confidentiality of communications made through the employee hotline or under the protection of the attorney-client privilege? On the one hand, if the organization promises to keep such communications confidential, is it ethical to breach that promise to protect the organization as a collective entity? On the other hand, to what extent is it ethical to expose the stockholders and other stakeholders to the risk of loss associated with corporate indictment and increased criminal penalties in order to honor the organization's commitment to individual employees, many of whom may have engaged in criminal wrongdoing? Can corporate managers honestly afford to tell employees that the organization will disclose any incriminating communications made to the "confidential" employee hotline or to corporate counsel under the protection of the attorney-client privilege whenever doing so is necessary to gain the benefits of cooperation under the Guidelines? If they do, will the organization be able to gather the information necessary to ensure that it is functioning ethically and in compliance with the law? Would any employee involved in an offense be willing to come forward? If not, how deceptive may the managers ethically be on this point?

Recall the second vignette from the beginning of this book. Stone Fund became aware of Gordon Gekko's illegal behavior when Budd Fox approached the organization's attorney for assurance that what he was doing for Gekko was legal. Fox spoke after being assured that his communications were protected by attorney-client privilege.

On learning that Gekko and Fox were engaged in criminal activity, what should Stone Fund's management do?

If it decides to fire Gekko but not report his and Fox's activities to the government, it exposes the organization to the risk of greatly enhanced penalties should the matter subsequently come to light. Stone Fund would lose the potential reductions to its culpability score for having an effective compliance program and for cooperation, and its score would be increased three points for its obstruction of justice. But the organization's managers cannot report Gekko's and Fox's activities to the government and disclose "all pertinent information known by the organization"[17] without waiving its attorney-client privilege and violating its promise of confidentiality to Fox. Assume again that you are one of the senior executives at Stone Fund. How sure are you that you know what constitutes ethical behavior under these circumstances?

11. Trust

Trust, unlike organizational justice, privacy, and confidentiality, does not embody an ethical principle. Although ethicists have argued that corporate managers who actively encourage their subordinates to trust them are thereby invested with positive moral obligations for the subordinates' well-being,[1] there is no independent moral obligation to trust others. Trust is nevertheless inextricably linked to ethical concerns because its existence in the workplace is dependent on the ethical behavior of corporate management. That is, unless corporate management meets its ethical obligations to its stakeholders and is perceived by them as doing so, no relationship of trust will develop or be maintained between the organization and its stakeholders.[2] And because the maintenance of such a relationship of trust is essential to the success of the organization,[3] trust serves as a necessary link between corporate performance and ethical behavior.

> Trust among stakeholders has become basic to the management of business firms in a competitive global economy. Trust leads to commitment, which results in effort, which is essential for success. But, trust can be generated only by treating members of the stakeholder groups in ways that they consider to be "right" and "just" and "fair." Treating groups in ways that can be considered to be "right" and "just" and "fair" is, of course, the domain of managerial ethics. . . .[4]

An organization's employees are one of its most important stakeholder groups. However, the personal interests of individual employees often diverge from the corporate interest of the organization. Consequently, businesses must expend resources to overcome the resulting commitment problems. In other words, the organization must align the incentives of its individual employees with the achievement of the organization's goals. But,

> [b]ecause these commitment problems (opportunism)
> abound, firms that solve commitment problems efficiently
> will have a competitive advantage over those that do not.
> Further, because ethical solutions to commitment problems
> are more efficient than mechanisms designed to curb oppor-
> tunism, it follows that *firms that contract (through their manag-*
> *ers) with their [employees] on the basis of mutual trust and coopera-*
> *tion will have a competitive advantage over firms that do not.*[5]

An organization that maintains a relationship of trust with its employees "will experience reduced agency costs, transaction costs, and costs associated with team production. More specifically, monitoring costs, bonding costs, search costs, warranty costs, and residual losses will be reduced... In such cases, overall contracting costs are reduced, and the benefits are shared among the firm and its stakeholders."[6] Hence, maintaining the trust of its employees can be crucial to an organization's competitive success.

Trust of the sort that can confer such advantages on organizations can develop only when three conditions are met: vulnerability, assumption of duty, and openness. First, trust requires vulnerability on the part of the trusting party. That is, "trust requires that firms and individuals expose their vulnerabilities to one another when there is clear uncertainty and risk that harm could come to the firm, or individuals in the firm, from those who are trusted."[7] Second, trust requires the trusted party to voluntarily and openly assume an obligation to protect the interests of the vulnerable party. In other words, "[t]rust is generally accompanied by an assumption of an acknowledged or accepted duty to protect the rights and interests of others [that gives rise to a]n expectation of generous or helpful or, at the very least, nonharmful behavior on the part of the trusted person, group, or firm. . . ."[8] Finally, trust requires openness. It depends "upon whether each [individual or firm] is prepared to open up to the other so as to reveal private or confidential information."[9] Such openness consists of "leveling with another, as well as not creating or permitting misleading expectations to be generated in the other."[10] Consequently, trust in the business environment has been defined as "the reliance by one person, group, or firm upon a voluntarily accepted duty on the part of another person, group, or firm to recognize and protect the rights and interests of all others engaged in a joint endeavor or economic exchange."[11]

The problem is that the incentives created by the law of white-collar crime are antithetical to the development of that form of trust. The standard for corporate criminal responsibility makes the organization strictly liable for the criminal offenses of its employees. The advent of broad new substantive, regulatory, and secondary offenses exponentially increases the chances that employees will either intentionally, negligently, or, in the case of public welfare offenses, innocently violate the law. The Organizational Sentencing Guidelines punish organizations that fail to aid in the prosecution of any of their employees whom the government suspects of committing an offense. These are hardly conditions that make it comfortable for organizations to repose significant amounts of trust in their employees or for the employees to feel secure in relying on the organization's commitment to protect their rights or interests. More specifically, these are conditions that undermine the second and third requirements for the development of trust.

The second requirement for trust is that organizations voluntarily and openly assume an obligation to protect the interests of their employees. By punishing organizations that honor this obligation in the context of a criminal investigation, the law of white-collar crime makes it extremely expensive for organizations to assume the necessary obligation. Employees obviously have interests in being accorded procedural justice and having their privacy respected and confidences maintained. But if an organization wants to avoid indictment and the prospect of greatly enhanced criminal punishment, it must sacrifice those interests to the government's interest in the efficient investigation and punishment of crime. Under the Organizational Sentencing Guidelines, assuming an obligation to protect employees' interests commits organizations to forgoing the culpability score reductions for effective compliance programs and cooperation and to risking the potential increase for obstruction of justice. Hence, in the current legal environment, trust comes at a very high price. But should an organization elect not to assume the obligation to protect its employees' interests in the context of a criminal investigation, trust will be considerably less likely to develop. It is very difficult for an organization to generate "an expectation of generous or helpful or, at the very least, nonharmful behavior"[12] toward its employees while it is aiding in their prosecution.[13]

The third requirement for trust is openness. It requires that an organization "level" with its employees and refrain from "creating or permitting misleading expectations to be generated"[14] about how the organization will behave with regard to its employees. If an organization leads or allows its employees to believe that it will afford them due process, respect their privacy, and maintain promised confidentiality and then fails to do so at the first hint of a criminal investigation, trust will be destroyed. For an organization to deal openly with its employees, it must either frankly inform them that it will fully cooperate with governmental efforts to prosecute them or, if the organization claims that it will not, make good on this claim and suffer the consequences of potential indictment and greatly enhanced penalties. Because the first of these alternatives amounts to a declaration that the organization will not protect its employees' interests, it is essentially equivalent to telling the employees not to trust the organization. Openly refusing to assume the obligation necessary to generate trust obviously will not generate trust. But the second alternative, which can generate trust, highlights how expensive trust becomes in the context of the federal government's campaign against white-collar crime.

Thus, the law of white-collar crime again places conscientious business managers in a difficult position. Because the trust of an organization's employees is an important business asset, the manager's obligation to the organization's stockholders and stakeholders requires the manager to try to maintain that trust. But the maintenance of employees' trust requires a commitment to precisely those forms of ethical organizational conduct (e.g., adhering to the standards of organizational justice, respecting employee privacy, and maintaining promised confidentiality) that the law of white-collar crime discourages. As a result, managers again find themselves forced to balance their ethical obligations against their obligation to fully comply with the law.

Because organizations are strictly liable for the offenses of their employees, the more trust managers invest in their employees, the more vulnerable they render their organizations to criminal sanction. The more managers trust their employees and refrain from directly monitoring their conduct, the easier it becomes for unscrupulous employees to commit criminal offenses for which the organization is liable. Additionally, that very trust will result in increased penalties for such offenses by preventing the organizations from receiving the culpability score reduction for effective compliance programs. However, the more managers take actions designed to guard against criminal liability and reduce potential penalties, the more they erode the culture of trust within their organizations. The very act of monitoring employees' conduct in order to detect and prevent the violations of law for which the organization will be held liable can generate a level of suspicion and invasion of privacy sufficient to undermine trust.[15] And to the extent that managers comply with the guidelines' incentives by sacrificing their employees' interests to the government's, they make it increasingly unlikely that employees will trust their motives in future dealings.

Thus, managers are once again called on to confront an array of difficult ethical choices. How much of their employees' trust should they be willing to sacrifice to protect the organization from potential legal liability? Is it ethical to expose the organization to the risk of indictment and enhanced criminal penalties in order to protect the interests of their individual employees sufficiently to generate trust? If an organization's management elects to ignore the guidelines' incentives in order to honor its ethical obligations to its employees, the organization must prevent its least scrupulous employees from violating the law. But because ferreting out potential criminals requires secret and potentially deceptive monitoring practices, how can management do this without thereby destroying the very trust that it is seeking to maintain?[16] And is it ethical to subject the majority of honest employees to this level of monitoring to protect the organization from the small minority of potential criminals?

Imagine again that you are a senior executive at Stone Fund when Budd Fox informs corporate counsel about Gordon Gekko and his activities. Should you fire Fox and report him to the Securities and Exchange Commission and the Department of Justice as the guidelines' standards for cooperation require? If you do, what will be the effect on your organization when word gets out that you took such action after Fox voluntarily came forward under a promise of confidentiality? To what extent will the organization's employees trust management's representations to them in the future? But, as the cases of Drexel Burnham Lambert and Arthur Andersen make clear, mere indictment could destroy a financial services company like Stone Fund.[17] Under such circumstances, is it ethical not to take every step prescribed by the Thompson Memorandum to avoid indictment? What precisely can you do to maintain a climate of trust within the organization without putting the very existence of the organization at risk?

12. Ethical Self-Assessment

It is possible that the different normative approaches to business ethics yield distinct sets of ethical obligations for managers. Although the stockholder, stakeholder, and social contract approaches coincide in prescribing the obligations to provide organizational justice, to respect privacy, and to maintain promised confidentiality, they may prescribe widely differing obligations in other respects. But whatever the precise configuration of managers' ethical obligations, managers are obviously required to make good-faith efforts to honor them. Such efforts require, at a minimum, that managers know what is going on within their organization.

Although this requirement may sound simple, in an organization of any considerable size, it is not. Many features of an organization's structure can impede the flow of information within the organization. Most large organizations are beset with what have been called "organizational blocks"—obstructions to information that result from "practices that are quite legitimate and inevitable in any complex organization,"[1] and that constitute the "unintended consequence[s] of organizational operating and control systems."[2] Thus, features such as the effect of strong role models in the organization, the strict line of command, the development of task group cohesiveness, the separation of decisionmaking authority, and the division of work between different units of the organization have all been identified as organizational blocks.[3]

The internal dynamics of individual advancement within organizations can also greatly hamper the flow of information. As individuals with different bits of knowledge seek to avoid blame for negative outcomes and claim credit for positive ones, information becomes increasingly distorted and nonspecific.[4] Indeed, the barriers to the free flow of information within organizations that arise because "[c]orporations compartmentalize knowledge, subdividing the elements of specific duties and operations into smaller components"[5] were the basis for the development of the collective knowledge standard for corporate criminal responsibility.[6]

This means that corporate managers cannot meet their obligation to ensure that their organization is functioning both ethically and legally merely by reviewing the information that reaches their desks. They must actively seek out the information necessary to form an accurate picture of what is taking place within their organization. Thus, organizations have a positive duty to engage in ethical and legal self-assessment.

Organizations usually go about fulfilling that duty in the ways touched upon in connection with the discussion of confidentiality.[7] To learn of potential ethical problems, organizations set up alternative, usually confidential, channels of communication that allow employees to voice ethical concerns without fear of damaging their careers. By using employee hotlines, ombudsmen, or ethics officers, organizations seek to circumvent both organizational blocks and the information-distorting effects of bureaucracy and personal interest. To learn of potential legal problems, organizations authorize their corporate counsel to gather information and conduct internal investigations under the protection of the attorney-client privilege. This allows organizations to avoid organizational blocks by going directly to the source of the information and to overcome the obscuring effects of self-interest by assuring employees that their statements to counsel will not be used against them at a later time. These mechanisms allow corporate managers to gather the information necessary to prevent or correct ethical lapses or legal violations.

The problem with this approach is that the law of white-collar crime makes engaging in such self-assessment a dangerous and potentially costly activity. Under the guidelines, any self-assessment that produces evidence suggestive of criminal activity would trigger a duty to immediately report the potential violation to the government and to fully cooperate in any resulting investigation, if the organization wishes to receive the culpability score reduction for cooperation. But because organizations are strictly liable for the offenses of their employees and because the reward for cooperation under the guidelines is not immunity from prosecution, but reduced penalties upon conviction,[8] organizations are placed in the position of having to aid in their own prosecution. There is considerably less incentive to undertake voluntary self-assessment when, by doing so, an organization may be developing the evidence that will lead to its conviction of a criminal offense. Furthermore, to receive the culpability score reduction for cooperation, organizations must disclose "all pertinent information known by the organization."[9] If this information was elicited by corporate counsel pursuant to the attorney-client privilege, disclosure will require waiver of the privilege. But because waiving the privilege with regard to any outside party waives it with regard to all outside parties—because the courts do not recognize the doctrine of selective waiver[10]—any information the organization discloses to the government will also be discoverable by private parties. As a result, an organization that undertakes a self-assessment is practically inviting civil litigation because any evidence of wrongdoing will be made public.

Once again, the law of white-collar crime creates a conflict for corporate managers. Ethically, they have a duty to undertake the type of self-assessment necessary to ensure that their organization is meeting its ethical and legal obligations. If they elect to undertake such an assessment, however, and then discover potential criminal activity, they must either reveal this information to the government, rendering the organization liable to both criminal penalties and civil damages awards, or conceal the information, rendering the organization liable to severely enhanced criminal penalties if the information subsequently comes to light. In contrast, if they do not undertake a self-assessment, there is a chance that any wrongdoing that may be occurring will never be discovered, and further, that if it later comes to light through the ordinary corporate reporting channels, the organization can cooperate with the government at that time. Under these circumstances, the least damaging course of action can appear to be to refrain from undertaking efforts at self-assessment at all.

Indeed, there is evidence that many organizations avoid formal self-assessment because they are aware that an organization that undertakes that task "can inadvertently land itself in serious legal trouble."[11] For example, a survey of major U.S. corporations undertaken by the Center for Effective Organizations at the University of Southern California suggested that organizational self-assessments are underused because corporate directors "are worried that any record of self-criticism might come back to haunt them in a shareholder suit or a government investigation" and "are fearful that [damaging] statements will show up in court proceedings (or be leaked to the press by plaintiffs' attorneys)."[12]

Think back to the third vignette at the beginning of this book. Imagine that you are the new chief executive officer of Endrun, trying to bring the company back from the brink of insolvency. Imagine further that the financial condition of the company has recently begun to improve and that you believe that if Endrun can weather the next six months, you may be able to return it to profitability. Although you have no reason to believe that any of Endrun's current employees are engaged in illegal activities, you are conscious of the fact that as a newcomer to the company, there may be things you are unaware of. Should you authorize an ethical or legal self-assessment? Is it even ethical to do so if you know that one more public scandal would destroy the company? Precisely what obligation do you have to undertake an ethical self-assessment when the discovery of any wrongdoing must be made public and can subject the corporation to criminal penalties and civil liability?

13. Conclusion

Let us return to the quiz in the opening pages. Viewed from a strictly legal perspective, it is now clear that the correct answer to all three questions is "e." Yet, it is doubtful whether many people would chose "e" as representing the ethically correct course of action.

Consider the first question on the quiz concerning Marsha Tudor. Legally speaking, "a" and "c" represent the most dangerous courses of action. In both cases, the CEO is electing not to meet the Thompson Memorandum's and Organizational Sentencing Guidelines' definition of cooperation, thereby subjecting the corporation to increased risk of indictment and significantly enhanced penalties if convicted. Further, if in aiding Marsha Tudor in her defense under "a" or in preparing the corporation's defense under "c," corporate counsel or anyone in corporate management suggests that any employee of Marsha Tudor Styles improperly assert his or her Fifth Amendment right or otherwise refrain from voluntarily cooperating with the government, the corporation risks the culpability score enhancement for obstruction of justice.

Both "b" and "d" are marginally better, but still dangerous, choices. With regard to "b," it is clearly false that the matter does not concern the corporation. Tudor is charged with securities fraud for attempting to prop up the value of MTS stock. As the chair of the board of directors of MTS, Tudor's conduct is clearly within the scope of her employment. Hence, MTS is strictly liable for her offense. By instructing the corporation to take no action, the CEO is, in essence, instructing it to refuse to cooperate with the government and thereby sacrificing the opportunity to lower the corporation's risk of being indicted and to reduce any potential penalties the corporation may incur. However, he or she is also making it less likely that the corporation will receive the culpability score enhancement for obstruction of justice. With regard to "d," the CEO's offer to cooperate with the government will be insufficient either to reduce the risk of indictment or to earn the culpability score reduction for cooperation. By acting to preserve the corporation's defenses and promises of confidentiality, the CEO is refusing to disclose all pertinent information possessed by MTS, and hence is failing to meet the Thompson Memorandum's and Sentencing Guidelines' definition of cooperation. The CEO's offer to cooperate in other respects, however, greatly reduces the chance that the corporation will receive the culpability score enhancement for obstruction of justice.

In electing any of the options "a" through "d," the CEO is essentially betting the corporation's interest on Tudor's exoneration, even though he or she is not sure that Tudor is innocent. Only "e" allows the corporation to improve its legal position regardless of the outcome of Tudor's case. By authorizing the corporation to plead guilty, the CEO is meeting the requirement that the corporation "clearly demonstrate[ ] recognition and affirmative acceptance of responsibility for its criminal conduct."[1] By waiving attorney-client privilege and turning over Tudor's records, the CEO is meeting the requirement that the corporation disclose "all pertinent information known by the organization."[2] And by turning over all relevant records in the corporation's possession, the CEO is ensuring that there can be no effort at concealment or alteration that could constitute obstruction of justice. These actions satisfy all the requirements for the five-point culpability score reduction for self-reporting, cooperation, and acceptance of responsibility, and they maximize the likelihood that the Department of Justice will decide not to indict the corporation. From a purely legal perspective, "e" is obviously the correct choice.

"E" is not obviously the ethically correct choice, however. Tudor founded and built the company, and her ongoing association with it has been a large factor in its continued success. Her hard work over the years has provided all employees of MTS with the opportunity for successful and rewarding careers. Under those circumstances, it is not unreasonable to believe that MTS owes her a duty of loyalty. There is certainly good reason to believe that it owes her at least the presumption of innocence and due process. In that case, from the ethical perspective, "a" is not necessarily an outlandish choice.

But perhaps there is no duty of loyalty in a business setting or, if there is, a corporate officer's duty to protect his or her company's other stakeholders overrides it. In that case, "b," and especially "c" and "d," may appear to be appropriate ethical choices. "E," on the other hand, is problematic. To the extent that Tudor communicated with corporate counsel under the promise of confidentiality inherent in the attorney-client privilege, the corporation's gratuitous disclosure of those communications to the government would constitute the ethical equivalent of fraud. Furthermore, by turning over to the government all records of Tudor's appointments, phone calls, and e-mails without regard to whether they contain job-related or purely personal information, the corporation may be violating Tudor's right to privacy. From an ethical perspective, "e" is almost certainly the wrong choice.

Now consider the second question on the quiz concerning Budd Fox. Legally speaking, "a" again represents the most dangerous choice. In the first place, the company is obviously sacrificing the five-point culpability score reduction for cooperation by aiding Fox in putting on a defense. It is also greatly increasing the likelihood that it will be indicted by ignoring the Thompson Memorandum's warning that, in deciding whether to bring an indictment, the DOJ will consider whether "the corporation appears to be protecting its culpable employees . . . either through the advancing of attorneys fees, through retaining the employees without sanction for their misconduct, or through providing information to the employees about the government's investigation pursuant to a joint defense agreement. . . ."[3] In addition, by retaining Fox without punishment, the company is sacrificing the three-point reduction for having an effective compliance program because, according to the Guidelines, "[a]dequate discipline of individuals responsible for an offense is a necessary component of [the] enforcement"[4] required for a compliance program to be considered effective. And, as in Tudor's case, if the company attempts to persuade any of its employees to refrain from voluntarily cooperating with the government, it risks the three-point enhancement for obstruction of justice.

Slightly better but still dangerous choices are "b," "c," and "d." Under "b," the company will still lose the reductions for having an effective compliance program by not disciplining or firing Fox and for cooperation by failing to satisfy the requirements of the Thompson Memorandum and Organizational Sentencing Guidelines, but it is unlikely to incur the enhancement for obstruction of justice.

Under "c" and "d," the company may gain the three-point reduction for its compliance program, but it is still sacrificing the opportunity to avoid indictment or receive the five-point reduction for cooperation by failing to actively aid in Fox's prosecution. Once again, "e," which offers the company an enhanced prospect of avoiding indictment altogether and of minimizing its fine if indicted and convicted, is the legally correct choice.

But again, "e" is not the ethically correct choice. Stone Fund hired Fox straight out of business school and placed him under the direction of one of the company's most powerful senior brokers, who was corrupt. By doing so, the company bears at least some responsibility for Fox's legal predicament. If Fox truly did not realize that he was engaged in illegal activity, especially if the company learned of Gekko's activities through Fox's queries to corporate counsel, he would have been acting as a loyal, if misguided, employee. Under these circumstances, it is entirely reasonable to believe that the principle of reciprocity imposes an ethical obligation on the company to help Fox deal with both his legal troubles and damaged career prospects. If so, then "a" may represent the ethically correct course for the company to take. But again, if one does not believe there is a duty of loyalty in business or if one believes that managers' obligations to the firm's stakeholders override any such duty, then "b," and perhaps "c" and "d," can appear to be ethically acceptable choices. Choices "c" and "d" may raise questions, however, because firing Fox—especially firing him and reporting his activities to the government—will almost certainly damage the level of trust within the company. Once the employees see that the company will sacrifice someone like Fox to protect its financial interests, they will be very unlikely to trust any future representation the company may make to protect their rights and interests. But "e" presents even more problems. By aiding in Fox's prosecution, the company is acting punitively toward an employee who is in trouble, at least in part, for following the directives of its senior management. It is also failing to honor the promise of confidentiality it extended with the attorney-client privilege. Such conduct makes it clear that the company cannot be relied on to protect the interests of its employees and will be destructive of the trust between employees and management that is so important to the successful functioning of a financial services company. Again, if one disregards its legal advantages, "e" is almost certainly the ethically wrong choice.

Finally, consider the question concerning Kevin Lie. From the legal perspective, there is little difference among choices "a," "b," "c," and "d." In none of those cases can Endrun expect to avoid indictment or receive a culpability score reduction on the basis of cooperation. To begin with, by covering Kevin Lie's legal expenses, the corporation is acting in a way that, under the Thompson Memorandum, indicates a lack of cooperation. Further, by preparing a defense or refusing to waive attorney-client privilege, the corporation is failing to disclose all pertinent information known to it, and thus, under the guidelines' definition, is failing to fully cooperate with the government. Finally, by putting on a defense, the corporation is failing to manifest the acceptance of responsibility necessary for a reduction in culpability score because the "adjustment is not intended to apply to an organization that puts the government to its burden of proof at trial by denying the essential factual elements of guilt."[5]

In contrast, "e" meets all legal requirements for cooperation. By indicating a willingness to plead guilty, Endrun is meeting the requirement for acceptance of responsibility. And by refusing to pay Lie's legal expenses, waiving attorney-client privilege, turning over all potentially relevant documents to the government, and otherwise aiding in Lie's prosecution, the corporation is meeting all of the other requirements of the Thompson Memorandum and the Organizational Sentencing Guidelines. These actions maximize Endrun's chances of avoiding indictment and of receiving the smallest possible fine if indicted and convicted. Thus, "e" is again the legally superior choice.

And once again, "e" is ethically the most questionable choice. In this case, it is not clear whether "a" is the ethically appropriate response. On the one hand, if the actions that Lie has been indicted for really represented his good-faith efforts to bring Endrun through a crisis, the corporation may have a duty of loyalty to help him defend himself. On the other hand, it may be argued that Lie brought his predicament on himself by hiring and failing to adequately supervise corrupt subordinates. If so, his negligence significantly damaged the company, and the company may owe him little loyalty and support. In this case, the ethically appropriate course of action may be either "b," "c," or "d." Regardless of whether Endrun owes Lie any active support, it owes him at least the presumption of innocence, which requires that Endrun meet its obligations to him until it has adequate evidence that he has behaved improperly. In other words, the company should honor both its promise to reimburse his legal expenses and its promise to keep his communications to corporate counsel confidential. Answers "b," "c," and "d" are all consistent with those obligations; "e" is not. Under "e," the corporation is denying Lie the presumption of innocence, abrogating its commitments to reimburse his legal expenses and maintain promised confidentiality, and helping the government circumvent Lie's constitutional right against self-incrimination by attempting to obtain and turn over to the government documents in his personal possession.[6] Discounting its legal effect, "e" is very unlikely to be the ethically proper course of conduct.

Those hypothetical cases show that, in the realm of white-collar crime, ethics and compliance are not coextensive. One can be acting in compliance with all legal requirements and incentives and still be behaving unethically, and one can be behaving ethically while failing to comply with various aspects of the law of white-collar crime. Fortunately, in most cases, ethical conduct and legal compliance do in fact coincide. But in an ever-increasing number of cases, the federal campaign against white-collar crime is directly at odds with the efforts of businesspeople to behave ethically.

Indeed, in business schools throughout the country, future MBAs are being taught that they have ethical obligations to their firms' employees and other stakeholders that can trump their firms' financial interest, and that effective management requires adherence to the principles of organizational justice and action that is productive of trust between a firm and its employees. Although the first and third of my hypothetical cases are obviously based on the Martha Stewart case and the Enron scandal, the second could be drawn from almost any contemporary business ethics course. In such a course, this case would be offered to show why "a" is the ethically correct course of conduct. Why this divergence between ethics and compliance?

Ethics is concerned with the moral desert. Ethically speaking, only morally blameworthy action should be punished. This is true of the traditional criminal law as well, which—with certain well-known exceptions,[7]—is designed to punish only those individuals who have acted in a morally culpable manner. The inherent liberalism of the traditional criminal law can be understood as the law's internal morality, an embedded code designed to ensure that the law remains true to that purpose. Viewed in this way, the ban on vicarious criminal liability and the requirement of a *mens rea* consisting of intentional or reckless conduct make perfect sense. So does the requirement of the principle of legality for clearly defined criminal offenses, because, for conduct that is not obviously *malum in se*, a person acts culpably only if he or she knows that that conduct is legally prohibited. And so do the procedural safeguards, which are designed to make it difficult for officials invested with the power to enforce the criminal law to use that power for purposes other than the punishment of morally culpable conduct. Hence, there is little divergence between ethics and compliance in the traditional criminal law because the law's inherent liberalism essentially writes ethics into the law.

In the beginning of this book, I defined the law of white-collar crime as the law designed to police the behavior of those parties involved in business for honest dealing and regulatory compliance. I might just as well have defined it as the body of criminal law that cannot be effectively enforced consistent with the law's internal morality. Although the inherent liberalism of the traditional criminal law keeps the law true to its purpose of punishing only morally culpable conduct, it does so by reducing the efficiency of governmental law enforcement efforts. In the context of an undertaking as monumentally difficult as policing the business environment of the entire United States for honest dealing and regulatory compliance, this reduction in efficiency is sufficient to render the law virtually unenforceable. Given this, it should be completely unsurprising that the development of the law of white-collar crime described in Part I of this book consisted of the evolution of various mechanisms for circumventing the liberal characteristics of the traditional criminal law. As both the courts and Congress have continually pointed out, doing so was the only way to prevent white-collar criminal law from becoming a dead letter.

The substantive protections provided by the ban on vicarious criminal liability, the *mens rea* requirement, and the principle of legality clearly had to be abandoned or relaxed if the statutes against white-collar crime were to be enforced. The Supreme Court explicitly recognized this necessity in creating corporate criminal responsibility, abandoning the ban on vicarious criminal liability purely on enforcement grounds—that is, because if "corporations may not be held responsible for and charged with the knowledge and purposes of their agents, . . . many offenses might go unpunished"[8] and because preserving the ban "would virtually take away the only means of effectually controlling the subject-matter and correcting the abuses aimed at."[9] The Court similarly justified the relaxation of the *mens rea* requirement to permit conviction for merely negligent, and even entirely innocent actions on the basis that, due to the "increasingly numerous and detailed regulations which heighten the duties of those in control of particular industries, trades, properties or activities that affect public health, safety or welfare,"[10] preserving the *scienter* requirement would "impair[ ] the efficiency of controls deemed essential to the social order as presently constituted."[11] Finally, the attenuation of the principle of legality necessary to permit the creation of vaguely defined, broad offenses such as mail fraud and RICO was justified on the grounds that such offenses were necessary to "cope with the new varieties of fraud that the ever-inventive American 'con artist' is sure to develop"[12] and "to bring criminal and other sanctions or remedies to bear on the unlawful activities of those engaged in organized crime and because the sanctions and remedies available to the Government are unnecessarily limited in scope and impact."[13]

Effective enforcement similarly required circumvention of the traditional law's procedural safeguards. Thus, the Court justified denying the Fifth Amendment privilege against self-incrimination not only to corporations but also to individuals subpoenaed in their capacity as employees of corporations on the ground that not doing so "would have a detrimental impact on the Government's efforts to prosecute 'white-collar crime,' one of the most serious problems confronting law enforcement authorities."[14] Secondary offenses such as money laundering, false statements, and obstruction of justice, which are designed solely to aid in law enforcement efforts, allow prosecutors to sidestep the requirement of proof beyond reasonable doubt by providing, in the words of two federal prosecutors, "the ability to prosecute a wrongdoer when there is either insufficient evidence of the underlying criminal conduct or insufficient evidence connecting the wrongdoer to the underlying criminal conduct."[15] Similarly, the presumption of innocence and the attorney-client privilege are compromised by the Organizational Sentencing Guidelines' culpability score adjustments for obstruction of justice, compliance programs, and cooperation, which, being specifically designed to aid law enforcement, effectively punish organizations that maintain their innocence or assert the privilege.

The law of white-collar crime, then, is that portion of the criminal law that has been significantly divorced from the law's internal morality. The essential purpose of white-collar criminal law is not the punishment of morally culpable conduct but the effective enforcement of congressionally created rules of behavior and regulations. To the extent that those rules and regulations prohibit conduct that is not clearly morally blameworthy, it is reasonable to expect the requirements of compliance with the law and the demands of ethics to diverge. And that is precisely what has happened.

As long as the imposition of criminal sanctions on organizations and individuals who commit white-collar offenses remains a priority, there is no way out of the dilemma this situation creates. Effective criminal enforcement requires the type of measures that create ethical dilemmas for conscientious businesspeople. Structuring the law to allow businesspeople to honor their ethical obligations would be equivalent to restoring the liberal characteristics of the traditional criminal law that render the law of white-collar crime unenforceable. But before simply accepting this state of affairs, it is worth considering whether the criminal punishment of those parties who commit white-collar offenses should remain a priority. For it is not clear how much is gained by such punishment.

White-collar criminal offenses consist in regulatory violations and deceptive or dishonest business practices not already punishable under the traditional criminal law. If the defendant is an organization, it can only be punished financially. If the organization is charged with an offense that consists of a breach of a regulation, it is already subject to a civil penalty for the violation. In such a case, a criminal conviction serves only to increase the amount of money that the organization must pay. But if a greater financial penalty is appropriate, the obvious thing to do is to increase the size of the civil penalty, not create a duplicative criminal offense. If the offense consists of deceptive or dishonest behavior by one of the organization's employees that results in a loss to the organization's stockholders or any other party, the organization is subject to a civil lawsuit and to the payment of compensatory and, if the conduct is intentional

93

or reckless, punitive damages. Once again, criminal punishment can only increase the amount of money that the organization must pay. And because this additional, purely punitive amount is paid by the organization's shareholders who are innocent of wrongdoing rather than by the actual guilty parties, it cannot be justified on retributive grounds.

One could argue that forcing organizations to pay an additional amount beyond the compensatory and punitive damages resulting from civil lawsuits is justified by its deterrent effect. The claim is that threatening the organization with additional monetary losses will make it more vigilant in supervising its employees to ensure that they do not engage in dishonest or deceptive behavior. There is reason to doubt this claim, however. Because the threat of civil liability already provides organizations with adequate incentives to properly supervise their employees, additional criminal liability can only be over-deterrence. Organizations are already strictly liable for the torts of their employees committed within the scope of their employment. Should an organization fail to exercise proper oversight to prevent deceptive or fraudulent practices by its employees, it can be made to pay not only compensatory damages but also potentially massive punitive damages. Further, because civil plaintiffs are not subject to the restrictions that the criminal law imposes on prosecutors, it is easier for them to establish liability. The type of complaints that civil plaintiffs may bring are not limited by the principle of legality, plaintiffs' efforts at discovery cannot be thwarted by a Fifth Amendment privilege, the defendant is not vested with a presumption of innocence that the plaintiff must overcome, and the plaintiff is not required to prove the elements of his or her case beyond reasonable doubt. It is difficult to see how the threat of additional criminal liability, which is more difficult to establish and, hence, less likely to be imposed, can increase the organization's vigilance. On the other hand, as the Arthur Andersen case demonstrates, because a criminal conviction can deplete the resources that an organization has available to pay civil judgments, the conviction can have the untoward effect of making it impossible for victims to recover their losses. Andersen had actually negotiated a $750 million settlement with Enron's shareholders that fell through when the firm was indicted.[16] Given the disparity between a $750 million settlement and the relatively small fine that can be levied for obstruction of justice, it is difficult to see what end is served by a criminal conviction that not only wipes out the firm's ability to compensate victims but also destroys the careers of thousands of Andersen employees who had nothing to do with the Enron case or the destruction of documents.

The situation may be different, however, when the defendant is an individual. Unlike organizations, individuals can be incarcerated. Perhaps the imprisonment of individuals who commit white-collar offenses serves important retributivist or deterrent ends. But then again, perhaps not.

When the offense is a public welfare offense that requires no *mens rea*, or an offense that requires only ordinary negligence, it is unclear how incarceration or punishment of any kind advances either end. Because the defendant has not acted in a morally blameworthy manner in committing such offenses, punishment cannot be justified on retributivist grounds. Further, because it was not the defendant's conscious plan to violate the regulation, the threat of punishment can have no deterrent effect. In such cases, the defendant may owe others or society compensation or the disgorgement of wrongfully acquired gains, but no legitimate end is served by his or her criminal punishment. And if a monetary payment is appropriate, it can be attained through the imposition of a civil penalty for the violation.

But what about individuals who intentionally violate regulations or engage in deceptive or dishonest business practices? In such cases, the defendants have acted culpably, meriting punishment, and can be deterred by the threat of incarceration. But here is where the perfect becomes the enemy of the good. Keep in mind that white-collar offenses consist of regulatory violations and deceptive or dishonest behavior that is not punishable under the traditional criminal law. The campaign against white-collar crime is not a campaign against actual fraud, which is already subject to punishment, but against the type of behavior that does not amount to actual fraud but is nevertheless unfair, deceptive, or dishonest. In essence, then, the purpose of the campaign against white-collar crime is to raise the ethical level of business behavior above the baseline supplied by the traditional criminal law.

Individuals who unfairly violate regulations or engage in deceptive or dishonest business practices do so for financial gain. If they are discovered, they will probably be discharged from their jobs and have their careers destroyed. If their conduct amounts to actual fraud, they will be subject to prosecution under the rules of the traditional criminal law. If it does not, they will be subject to civil lawsuits that will cause them to at least give up all ill-gotten gains and that probably will impoverish them. Hence, the market and civil liability sanctions against such individuals are considerable.

Because the imposition of additional financial penalties on such individuals would be pointless, the effort to subject them to the criminal sanction can only be for purposes of incarceration. Such punishment can be justified on retributive grounds if the market and civil liability sanctions are truly insufficient relative to the defendants' culpability. It can also be justified on deterrent grounds if the threat of imprisonment would discourage at least some individuals who would not be deterred by the prospect of the loss of their careers and wealth. It must be conceded, however, that the gain in either retributive or deterrent value, although real, is relatively small.

But at what cost are these gains purchased? The answer to this question has been the subject of this book. The cost of this crusade to achieve perfect justice is the abandonment of the internal morality of the criminal law and the ethical dilemmas it imposes on the business community. It appears that in order to use the criminal law to raise the ethical level of business behavior among those parties given to unscrupulous action, we must incentivize unethical behavior on the part of those who are conscientious. This is a textbook example of a Pyrrhic victory. Here truly is a game that is not worth the candle.

Given this situation, let me conclude the book with the thought that the solution to the problem of white-collar crime simply does not lie with more vigorous federal enforcement efforts. Such efforts may well be justified with regard to crimes that directly harm or violate the rights of others. But the criminal sanction is too blunt an instrument to be efficient in either raising the general level of honest dealing in business or effectively increasing compliance with *malum prohibitum* regulations. Hence, with regard to this category of offense, the proper solution may lie in abstaining from any efforts at criminal enforcement at all.

Notes

Chapter 1

1. U.S. Sentencing Comm'n, Guidelines Manual ch. 8 (2004) [hereinafter U.S.S.G.], *available at* http://www.ussc.gov/2004guid/CHAP8.pdf.

Chapter 2

1. Edwin H. Sutherland, White Collar Crime: The Uncut Version 7 (1983) (explaining that "[w]hite-collar crime may be defined approximately as a crime committed by a person of respectability and high social status in the course of his occupation.").

2. James W. Coleman, *Toward an Integrated Theory of White-Collar Crime*, 93 Am. J. Soc. 406, 407 (1987) (finding that white-collar crime consists of illegal acts by individuals or groups who are otherwise conducting legal and respectable business).

3. Susan P. Shapiro, *Collaring the Crime, Not the Criminal: Reconsidering the Concept of White-Collar Crime*, 55 Am. Soc. Rev. 346, 346 (1990) (arguing that "white collar criminals violate norms of trust, enabling them to rob without violence and burgle without trespass.").

4. U.S. Dep't of Justice, Attorney General's Report (1983) ("White Collar Crimes are illegal acts that use deceit and concealment—rather than the application or threat of physical force or violence—to obtain money, property, or service; to avoid the payment or loss of money; or to secure a business or personal advantage."); Bureau of Justice Statistics, U.S. Dep't of Justice, Dictionary of Criminal Justice Data Terminology 215 (2d ed. 1981) ("[N]onviolent crime for financial gain utilizing deception and committed by anyone having special technical and professional knowledge of business and government, irrespective of the person's occupation.").

5. See J. Hamelkamp, R. Ball, and K. Townsend (eds.), *Definitional Dilemma: Can and Should There Be a Universal Definition of White Collar Crime?* Proceedings of the Academic Workshop (Morgantown, WV: National White Collar Crime Center Training and Research Institute, 1996) 330 (describing white collar crime as "[i]llegal or unethical acts that violate fiduciary responsibility or public trust, committed by an individual or organization, usually during the course of legitimate occupational activity, by persons of high or respectable social status for personal or organizational gain.").

6. See Harry First, First's Business Crime: Cases and Materials v (1990).

7. *E.g.*, M.G.L.A. 266 § 30 (2004) (Larceny; General Provisions and Penalties); Md. Code Ann., [Crim. Law] § 7-109 (2004) (Crimes Including Theft); Va. Code Ann. § 18.2-178 (2004) (False Pretenses); W.Va. Code § 61-3-24 (2004) (Crimes Against Property).

8. People v. Drake, 462 N.E.2d 376, 377 (N.Y. 1984).

9. See Wayne R. LaFave, Criminal Law 957 (4th ed. 2003) (explaining that "[f]alse pretenses, a statutory crime, although defined in slightly different ways in the various jurisdictions, consists in most jurisdictions of five elements: (1) a false representation

of a material present or past fact (2) which causes the victim (3) to pass title to (4) his property to the wrongdoer, (5) who (a) knows his representation to be false and (b) intends thereby to defraud the victim."); HOWARD G. LEVENTHAL, 1 CHARGES TO THE JURY AND REQUESTS TO CHARGE IN A CRIMINAL CASE, NEW YORK § 50:2 (2004) (noting that the "elements of proof required to establish larceny by false pretenses are: (a) criminal intent to deprive the owner of property; (b) that defendant made a false representation of a past or existing fact; (c) that defendant knew the representation was false when made; (d) that defendant obtained property of another; and (e) that the representation was believed and relied on by the person to whom made and that person was in whole or in part induced thereby to give his property to the defendant.").

10. 18 U.S.C. § 1341 (2004).

11. *Id.; see also* United States v. Lopez-Lukis, 102 F.3d 1164, 1168 (11th Cir. 1997) ("[T]he Government must prove that the defendants '(1) intentionally participated in a scheme or artifice to defraud and (2) used the United States mails to carry out that scheme or artifice.'").

12. *See* 18 U.S.C. § 1346 (defining the terms "Scheme or Artifice to Defraud" in the Code).

13. *See* Neder v. United States, 527 U.S. 1, 24–25 (1999) (holding that "[t]he common-law requirements of 'justifiable reliance' and 'damages,' for example, plainly have no place in the federal fraud statutes.").

14. *See* United States v. Brown, 79 F.3d 1550 (11th Cir. 1996).

15. *See* United States v. Jain, 93 F.3d 436 (8th Cir. 1996).

Chapter 3

1. Actually, criminal culpability required not merely *mens rea*, but also the convergence of *actus reus* and *mens rea*. This combination meant that the state could punish for neither actions nor thoughts alone. Like the *mens rea* requirement, the *actus reus* requirement serves a civil liberty by preventing the state from pursuing "thought crimes" and criminalizing unpopular religious, political, or cultural beliefs. Although this feature of the criminal law is highly relevant in the context of attempt and other inchoate crimes, *see, e.g.,* John Hasnas, *Once More Unto the Breach: The Inherent Liberalism of the Criminal Law and Liability for Attempting the Impossible*, 54 HASTINGS L.J. 1, 57–61 (2002), it is not of central relevance in the context of white-collar crime.

2. Arnold N. Enker, *Impossibility in Criminal Attempts—Legality and the Legal Process*, 53 MINN. L. REV. 665, 668 (1969).

3. *See* JOSHUA DRESSLER, UNDERSTANDING CRIMINAL LAW 115 (3d ed. 2001) (discussing the history of *mens rea* and the ambiguity inherent in the concept, making it hard to define and prove).

4. One could be prosecuted as an accomplice, of course, but that was for one's own actions in aiding or abetting another's criminal activity.

5. Francis B. Sayre, *Criminal Responsibility for the Acts of Another: Development of the Doctrine Respondeat Superior*, 43 HARV. L. REV. 689, 702 (1930).

6. *Id.* at 694. The possible exceptions to this rule in England were criminal nuisance and libel. However, neither of those exceptions applied in the United States. LAFAVE, *supra* chapter 2, note 9, at 695 n.5.

7. LAFAVE, *supra* chapter 2, note 9, at 11; *see also* JEROME HALL, GENERAL PRINCIPLES OF CRIMINAL LAW 28 (2d ed. 1960) (stating that conduct is only criminal if it is described in criminal law); GLANVILLE WILLIAMS, CRIMINAL LAW: THE GENERAL PART 575 (2d ed.

1961) (defining the principle of legality as the concept that crime and punishment must be in accordance with the law).

8. *See* LaFave, *supra* chapter 2, note 9, at 11 (illuminating these four corollaries and their effect on American laws); *see also* Dressler, *supra* note 3, at 39–40 (describing in detail the principle of *nullum crimen sine lege, nulla poena sine lege*).

9. Dressler, *supra* note 3, at 39.

10. Herbert Packer, The Limits of the Criminal Sanction 80 (1968).

11. *See, e.g.*, Model Penal Code § 1.12(1) (2004) (stating that "[n]o person may be convicted of an offense unless each element of such offense is proved beyond a reasonable doubt. In the absence of such proof, the innocence of the defendant is assumed.").

12. 4 William Blackstone, Commentaries on the Laws of England 352 (1765).

13. Coffin v. United States, 156 U.S. 432, 453 (1895).

14. *In re* Winship, 397 U.S. 358, 364 (1970). Other procedural features such as the right to trial by a jury in which conviction requires a unanimous verdict further reinforce the liberal bias of the criminal law. *Id.*

15. *See* Swidler & Berlin v. United States, 524 U.S. 399, 403 (1998) (describing the attorney-client privilege as one of the oldest recognized rights).

16. U.S. Const. amend. V.

17. Jerold H. Israel & Wayne R. LaFave, Criminal Procedure 26 (1985).

18. *See* Leonard W. Levy, The Origins of the Fifth Amendment: The Right Against Self-Incrimination 332 (1986) (Oxford U. Press 1968).

The right implied a humane or ethical standard in judging a person accused of a crime, regardless how heinous the crime or strong the evidence of his guilt. It reflected consideration for the human personality in that respect, but it also reflected the view that society benefited by seeking his conviction without the aid of his involuntary admissions. Forcing self-incrimination was thought not only to brutalize the system of criminal justice but to produce weak and untrustworthy evidence.

Above all, the right was most closely linked to freedom of religion and speech. . . In the broadest sense it was a protection not of the guilty, or of the innocent, but of freedom of expression, of political liberty, of the right to worship as one pleased. In sum, its subtle and slow emergence in English law was, in the words of Dean Erwin N. Griswold, "one of the great landmarks of man's struggle to make himself civilized," "an expression of the moral striving of the community," and "an ever-present reminder of our belief in the importance of the individual."

Id. (quoting Erwin N. Griswold, The 5th Amendment Today; Three Speeches 1 (1955)).

19. Israel & LaFave, *supra* note 17, at 26.

20. United States v. Bank of New England, 821 F.2d 844, 856 (1st Cir. 1987).

21. United States v. Hilton Hotels Corp., 467 F.2d 1000, 1006 (9th Cir. 1972).

22. United States v. Maze, 414 U.S. 395, 407 (1974) (Burger, C.J., dissenting).

23. *Id.*

24. *Id.* at 406 (commenting on how the Mail Fraud Statute is a stop-gap for new criminal activity, giving time for Congress to develop new laws for new types of fraud).

25. *See id.* at 405–08 (mentioning the burden placed on Congress to enact laws quickly enough to counteract new types of white-collar crime).

26. *See* Hazel Croall, Understanding White Collar Crime 1 (Mike Maguire ed. 2001).

27. By secondary offenses, I mean offenses such as money laundering, 18 U.S.C. §§ 1956–1967 (2004); obstruction of justice, 18 U.S.C. §§ 1503, 1505, 1510, 1512; and false statements, 18 U.S.C. § 1001, which consist of conduct that makes it more difficult for the government to succeed in the prosecution of other substantive offenses.

28. U.S.S.G., *supra* chapter 1, note 1, ch. 8.

Chapter 4

1. 212 U.S. 481 (1909).

2. 49 U.S.C. §§ 41–43 (1976), *repealed by* Pub. L. 95-473, 92 Stat. 1466, 1467–70 (1978).

3. *New York Central*, 212 U.S. at 492.

4. *Id.*

5. *Id.* at 493.

6. *Id.*

7. *Id.* at 494.

8. *Id.* at 494–95.

9. *Id.* at 495–96.

10. 467 F.2d 1000 (9th Cir. 1972).

11. 15 U.S.C. § 1 (2004) (prohibiting contracts or conspiracies to restrain interstate commerce or trade).

12. *See Hilton Hotels*, 467 F.2d at 1004 (adding that the purchasing agent's decision to violate Hilton Hotel's policy resulted from "anger and personal pique toward the individual representing the supplier.").

13. *Id.* at 1007.

14. *Id.* at 1006.

15. 821 F.2d 844 (1st Cir. 1987).

16. *Id.* at 855.

17. 31 U.S.C. § 5322 (2001).

18. *See Bank of New England*, 821 F.2d at 846 (summarizing the bank's conviction of 31 violations of the Currency Transaction Reporting Act, which requires a bank to file a Currency Transaction Report within 15 days of customer transactions greater than $10,000).

19. *Id.* at 855 (quoting the trial judge's explanation of collective knowledge).

20. *Id.*

21. *Id.* at 856 (quoting United States v. T.I.M.E.-D.C., Inc., 381 F. Supp. 730, 738 (W.D. W. Va. 1974)).

22. Actually, the corporation is often required to ensure that none of its employees negligently breaks the law as well. *See infra* text accompanying chapter 5, notes 45–48.

23. *See supra* text accompanying chapter 3, notes 20–21.

24. 201 U.S. 43, 74 (1906) (stating, "[W]e are of the opinion that there is a clear distinction in this particular between an individual and a corporation, and that the latter has no right to refuse to submit its books and papers for an examination at the suit of the state."); *see also* Braswell v. United States, 487 U.S. 99, 105 (1988) (explaining that "*Hale* settled that a corporation has no Fifth Amendment privilege.").

25. ISRAEL & LAFAVE, *supra* chapter 3, note 17, at 26.

26. *Braswell*, 487 U.S. at 104.

27. *Id.* at 108–09.

28. *Id.* at 115. Ironically, in the earlier case of *Bellis v. United States*, the Court justified its refusal to allow individuals to assert their Fifth Amendment privilege

with respect to corporate documents on the grounds that "recognition of the individual's claim of privilege with respect to the financial records of the organization would substantially undermine the unchallenged rule that the organization itself is not entitled to claim any Fifth Amendment privilege, and largely frustrate legitimate governmental regulation of such organizations." 417 U.S. 85, 90 (1974). Thus, the very existence of the theoretically ungrounded collective entity rule is offered as a justification for denying individuals the protection of the right against self-incrimination, as is the fact that if it is not curtailed, the right would effectively perform its intended function of limiting the means by which the government may exercise its regulatory power.

Chapter 5

1. It has been noted, for example, that "[d]uring the past century, both Congress and the Supreme Court have repeatedly placed their stamps of approval on expansive use of the mail fraud statute. Indeed, each of the five legislative revisions of the statute has served to enlarge its coverage." Jed S. Rakoff, *The Federal Mail Fraud Statute (Part I)*, 18 Duq. L. Rev. 771, 772 (1980).

2. 18 U.S.C. §§ 1961–63 (2003).

3. 18 U.S.C. §§ 1341, 1346 (2002).

4. *See supra* chapter 2, notes 10–15 and accompanying text (explaining the requirements for the crime of mail fraud and its implications in practice). The comments that follow should be understood as applying to wire fraud, 18 U.S.C. § 1343; bank fraud, 18 U.S.C. § 1344; health care fraud, 18 U.S.C. § 1347; and securities fraud, 18 U.S.C. § 1348, as well as to mail fraud. The requirement of a scheme or artifice to defraud is common to them all.

5. *See supra* chapter 2, note 9.

6. Kevin F. O'Malley et al., Federal Jury Practice and Instructions § 47.13 (5th ed. 2000).

7. 18 U.S.C. § 1346.

8. *Neder*, 527 U.S. at 25.

9. *Id.* at 24–25.

10. United States v. Townley, 665 F.2d 579, 585 (5th 1982). The prosecution must also establish the use of the mails, but this stipulation requires neither that United States mails actually be used nor that the message sent be false or misleading in any way. The mailing may be sent either by the U.S. Postal Service or by "any private or commercial interstate carrier," 18 U.S.C. §1341, and "[i]t is sufficient for the mailing to be 'incidental to an essential part of the scheme,' or 'a step in the plot.'" Schmuck v. United States, 489 U.S. 705, 710–11 (1989). Thus, "'innocent' mailings—ones that contain no false information—may supply the mailing element . . . [and] the Court has found the elements of mail fraud to be satisfied where the mailings have been routine." *Id.* at 715.

11. United States v. Rybicki, 287 F.3d 257, 264 (2d Cir. 2002).

12. *Id.*

13. United States v. Brown, 79 F.3d 1550 (11th Cir. 1996); *see supra* chapter 2, note 14 and accompanying text (discussing *Brown* as an example of the coverage of the mail fraud statute).

14. United States v. Jain, 93 F.3d 436 (8th Cir. 1996); *see supra* chapter 2, note 15 and accompanying text (analyzing *Jain* as an example of the extent of the mail fraud statute).

15. United States v. Lopez-Lukis, 102 F.3d 1164, 1165 (11th Cir. 1997) (charging defendant under the mail fraud statute for "depriv[ing] the citizens . . . of Florida of their intangible right to [the defendant's] honest services . . . in her capacity as Lee County Commissioner.").

16. United States v. D'Amato, 39 F.3d 1249 (2d Cir. 1994).

17. United States v. Czubinski, 106 F.3d 1069 (1st Cir. 1997). This case involved a conviction for wire fraud rather than mail fraud.

18. Indictment, United States v. Stewart, No. 03 Cr. 717, ¶ 60–61 (S.D.N.Y. June 4, 2003), *available at* http://news.findlaw.com/hdocs/docs/mstewart/usmspb60403ind.pdf.

19. *Id.* ¶ 60.

20. *Id.* ¶ 57.

21. *Id.* ¶ 60.

22. Rakoff, *supra* note 1, at 771.

23. *See* 18 U.S.C. §§ 1961–1962 (2000) (defining "racketeering activity" under the various RICO provisions, and prohibiting activities defined as racketeering).

24. *See* 18 U.S.C. § 1962(d) (dictating that it is unlawful to conspire to violate RICO-prohibited activities).

25. *See* 18 U.S.C. § 1961 (defining racketeering activity to include mail fraud, wire fraud, and financial institution fraud).

26. Organized Crime Control Act of 1970, Pub. L. 91-452, 84 Stat. 922, 923 (1970).

27. *See* 84 Stat. at 947 (indicating that liberal construction is necessary to serve RICO's remedial purpose).

28. *See* Sedima v. Imrex Co., 473 U.S. 479, 497–98 (1985).

29. *See* United States v. Turkette, 452 U.S. 576, 576 (1981).

30. *See* Terrance G. Reed, *The Defense Case for RICO Reform*, 43 VAND. L. REV. 691, 700–01 (1990).

31. The common law did, on occasion, permit "strict liability" with regard to legally required attendant circumstances when the act the defendant engaged in was inherently wrong. *See* Regina v. Prince, 2 L.R.-C.C.R. 154 (Crown Cases Reserved 1875). Thus, if one intentionally had intercourse with a young girl, it was not a defense to a charge of statutory rape that one did not know she was underage. *See* People v. Olsen, 685 P.2d 52, 57 (Cal. 1984). However, the fact that neither knowledge nor negligence with regard to an attendant circumstance was required does not imply the offense was one of strict liability. The defendant was still required to intentionally produce the prohibited consequence. Thus, in the case of statutory rape, the defendant had to intentionally engage in the act of intercourse. *Id.* at 59.

32. *See, e.g.*, Commonwealth v. Welansky, 55 N.E.2d 902, 911 (Mass. 1944) (noting that "[t]here is in Massachusetts at common law no such thing as 'criminal negligence.' ").

33. *See* State v. Barnett, 63 S.E.2d 57, 58–59 (S.C. 1951).

34. *Id.* at 59. The Model Penal Code defines criminal negligence as involving a risk "of such a nature and degree that the actor's failure to perceive it, considering the nature and purpose of his conduct and the circumstances known to him, involves a gross deviation from the standard of care that a reasonable person would observe in the actor's situation." MODEL PENAL CODE § 2.02 (2)(d) (Proposed Official Draft 1962).

35. *See* Morissette v. United States, 342 U.S. 246, 256 (1952) (upholding a statute punishing public welfare offenses that did not require a criminal intent).

36. *Id.* at 254.

37. *Id.* at 256.

38. *Id.*

39. *Id.*

40. *Id.* (providing that the public welfare doctrine applies where "penalties commonly are relatively small, and conviction does no grave damage to an offender's reputation.").

41. Rivers and Harbors Act of 1899 § 13, 33 U.S.C. § 407 (1899) (making it illegal to discharge any type of refuse other than what flows from streets and sewers into any "navigable" water in the United States).

42. United States v. White Fuel Corp., 498 F.2d 619, 621 (1st Cir. 1974).

43. *See id.* at 623 (explaining that society receives great benefit from easily defined, easily enforceable statutes).

44. *Id.*

45. *See* 33 U.S.C. § 1321 (b)(3) (prohibiting any discharge of oil or other hazardous material into the water of the United States).

46. United States v. Hanousek, 176 F.3d 1116, 1119–20, 1126 (9th Cir. 1999).

47. Steven P. Solow & Ronald A. Sarachan, *Criminal Negligence Prosecutions Under the Federal Clean Water Act: A Statistical Analysis and the Evaluation of the Impact of Hanousek and Hong*, 32 ENVTL. L. REP. 11,153, 11,155 (2002).

48. *Hanousek*, 176 F.3d at 1121. Although *Hanousek* is a rather recent decision, federal prosecutors have long presumed that the intent standard for the Clean Water Act is simple negligence. Solow & Sarachan, *supra* note 47, at 11, 159. Furthermore, the courts have endorsed the prosecution of corporate officials for the ordinary negligence of their subordinates when those officials are responsible corporate officers. United States v. Hong, 242 F.3d 528, 531 (4th Cir. 2001). In *Hong*, the court found that officers who have the responsibility and authority to prevent or correct a violation by virtue of their position in the corporation can be criminally liable for actions of their subordinates. United States v. Park, 421 U.S. 658, 673–74 (1975).

49. 31 U.S.C. § 5322 (2000) makes it a felony to willfully fail to file required currency transaction reports (CTRs). 31 U.S.C. § 1313 requires banks and financial institutions to report transactions of more than $10,000. 31 U.S.C. § 1316 requires casinos and persons moving currency in and out of the country to report transactions or currency movements of more than $10,000. 26 U.S.C. § 6050I(a) requires all persons receiving more than $10,000 in cash in the course of one's business to file a report. 31 U.S.C. § 5324 makes it a felony for anyone to structure his or her financial transactions to avoid federal reporting requirements.

50. § 1956(a)(1)(B)(i).

51. 935 F.2d 832 (7th Cir. 1991).

52. *Id.* at 841.

53. *See* 18 U.S.C. § 1957(a).

54. *See* United States v. Moore, 27 F.3d 969, 976 (4th Cir. 1994) (holding that the government does not have to prove that no untainted funds were involved in the transaction if the transaction originated from a single source of commingled lawful and unlawful money); see also United States v. Johnson, 971 F.2d 562, 570 (10th Cir. 1992) (noting that if the government was required to prove that no untainted funds were used, individuals could avoid prosecution by commingling illegitimate and legitimate funds).

55. *See* 18 U.S.C. § 1957(f)(1) (indicating that "the term 'monetary transaction' . . . does not include any transaction necessary to preserve a person's right to representation as guaranteed by . . . the Constitution.").

56. The secondary offense, incidentally, often carries a greater penalty than the underlying substantive offense. *See* NORMAN ABRAMS & SARAH SUN BEALE, FEDERAL CRIMINAL LAW AND ITS ENFORCEMENT 397–98 (3d ed. 2000) (explaining that the sentence for money laundering is almost four times greater than for the crime that generates the unlawful proceeds).

57. *See* Brogan v. United States, 522 U.S. 398, 400 (1998).

58. *Id.* at 405.

59. *See* 18 U.S.C. §§ 1503, 1505, 1510, 1512, 1519–1520 (listing the various obstruction of justice offenses).

60. Indictment, United States v. Arthur Andersen, LLP, No. H-02-121, 2002 WL 32153945 (S.D. Tex. Mar. 14, 2002).

61. Government's Memorandum of Law in Opposition to Andersen's Motion for a Judgment of Acquittal or a New Trial, United States v. Arthur Andersen LLP, (S.D. Tex. 2002) (Cr. No. H-02-121) *in* JULIE R. O'SULLIVAN, FEDERAL WHITE COLLAR CRIME 458 (2d ed. 2003).

Arthur Andersen's conviction was subsequently overturned by the Supreme Court because the jury instructions did not require the consciousness of wrongdoing that the Court found to be demanded by the statutory language requiring the defendant to "knowingly . . . corruptly persuad[e]" another. Although this ruling thereby strengthened the *mens rea* requirement of § 1512, it did not narrow the range of its application described above.

In fact, the Court's ruling in Arthur Andersen v. United States, 125 S.Ct. 2129 (2005), undermines none of the points made in this book about the scope of the obstruction of justice statutes. Only § 1512 requires knowing, corrupt persuasion for conviction; § 1519, which was enacted as part of the Sarbanes-Oxley Act of 2002, does not require corrupt motivation but merely that one "*knowingly* alters, destroys, mutilates, conceals, covers up, falsifies, or makes a false entry in any record, document, or tangible object with the intent to impede, obstruct, or *influence* the investigation or proper administration of any matter within the jurisdiction of any department or agency within the United States . . ." (emphasis added). Thus, although the Supreme Court's ruling in *Andersen* means that no individual or corporation can now be convicted under § 1512 of corruptly persuading another to obstruct justice without a showing of consciousness of wrongdoing, one may still be convicted of obstruction of justice under § 1519 without such a showing. Thus, for all prosecutorial intents and purposes, § 1512 has been superceded by § 1519.

For this reason, I believe it is entirely appropriate to retain the Arthur Andersen case as illustrative of the scope of the obstruction of justice statutes, and I have chosen to do so.

62. Indictment, United States v. Quattrone, No. 03 Cr., ¶¶ 27–28 (S.D.N.Y. May 12, 2003) (charging Quattrone with obstruction of justice for promoting file destruction), *available at* http://news.findlaw.com/hdocs/docs/csfb/usquattrone 51203ind.pdf.

63. *See* United States v. O'Hagan, 521 U.S. 642, 651–52 (1997).

64. Despite the impression given by press accounts of the verdict, Stewart was not convicted for lying about whether she sold her Imclone stock pursuant to a stop-loss order. United States v. Martha Stewart, 323 F. Supp. 2d 606, 609 (S.D.N.Y. 2004). Specifically,

[t]he jury found Stewart guilty of making the following false statements, each of which was a specification in Count Three of the Indictment. Stewart told the Government investigators that she spoke to Bacanovic on December 27 and

instructed him to sell her ImClone shares after he informed her that ImClone was trading below $60 per share. Stewart also stated that during the same telephone call, she and Bacanovic discussed the performance of the stock of her own company, Martha Stewart Living Omnimedia ("MSLO"), and discussed K-Mart. She told investigators that she had decided to sell her ImClone shares at that time because she did not want to be bothered during her vacation. Stewart stated that she did not know if there was any record of a telephone message left by Bacanovic on December 27 in her assistant's message log. She also said that since December 28, she had only spoken with Bacanovic once regarding ImClone, and they had only discussed matters in the public arena. Finally, Stewart told investigators that since December 28, Bacanovic had told her that Merrill Lynch had been questioned by the SEC regarding ImClone, but that he did not tell her that he had been questioned by the SEC or that he had been questioned about her account.

The jury acquitted Stewart of one specification charged in Count Three: her statement that she and Bacanovic had agreed, at a time when ImClone was trading at $74 per share, that she would sell her shares when ImClone started trading at $60 per share.

Id.

65. United States v. Maze, 414 U.S. 395, 405–06 (Burger, C.J., dissenting).

66. Rakoff, *supra* note 1, at 772.

67. *See* United States v. Rybicki, 354 F.3d 124, 163–64 (2d Cir. 2003) (Jacobs, J., dissenting) (intimating that the issue may be ripe for consideration by the Supreme Court because

the vagueness of the statute has induced court after court to undertake a rescue operation by fashioning something that (if enacted) would withstand a vagueness challenge. The felt need to do that attests to the constitutional weakness of section 1346 as written. And the result of all these efforts—which has been to create different prohibitions and offenses in different circuits—confirms that the weakness is fatal. Judicial invention cannot save a statute from unconstitutional vagueness; courts should not try to fill out a statute that makes it an offense to "intentionally cause harm to another," or to "stray from the straight and narrow," or to fail to render "honest services.").

68. United States v. Rybicki, 354 F.3d 124, 141 (2d Cir. 2003).

69. *Id.* at 141–42.

70. *Id.* at 164 (Jacobs, J., dissenting).

71. *Id.* at 161.

72. *Id.*

73. *Id.*

74. *See* Cheek v. United States, 498 U.S. 192, 201–02 (1991) (finding that the willful conduct requirement of 26 U.S.C. § 7201 (1982) requires the government to prove the defendant knew his actions violated the statute).

75. Enker, *supra* chapter 3, note 2, at 668.

76. *Id.*

77. *See supra* text accompanying notes 62–64.

78. B. Frederick Williams, Jr., & Frank D. Whitney, Federal Money Laundering: Crimes and Forfeitures 14–16 (1999). Other advantages the authors mention include the ability to introduce potentially prejudicial evidence of wealth and "big spending"

at trial and the ability to avoid the statute of limitations on the underlying offense by charging a defendant with a recent monetary transaction. *Id.* at 15.

79. 983 F.2d 757, 766–67 (7th Cir. 1993); *see supra* note 51 and accompanying text.

80. This conclusion remains true even after the Supreme Court's decision in Arthur Andersen v. United States, 125 S.Ct. 2129 (2005), as long as the prosecution can establish that the persuader was conscious that he or she was acting wrongfully. *See supra* note 61.

Chapter 6

1. U.S. SENTENCING COMM'N, GUIDELINES MANUAL ch. 8 (1991). The recent amendments to the Sentencing Guidelines became effective on November 1, 2004. *See* U.S.S.G., *supra* chapter 1, note 1, app. C (2004) (amendment 673).

2. *Id.* § 8C2.7.

3. *Id.* § 8C2.4(a).

4. *Id.* § 8C2.4(d).

5. JED S. RAKOFF ET AL., CORPORATE SENTENCING GUIDELINES: COMPLIANCE AND MITIGATION § 1.05[3] (1993).

6. U.S.S.G., *supra* chapter 1, note 1, § 8C2.5.

7. *Id.* § 8C2.5(e).

8. *Id.* § 8C2.5(f).

9. *Id.* § 8C2.5(g)(1).

10. RAKOFF ET AL., *supra* note 5, § 2.06.

11. U.S.S.G., *supra* chapter 1, note 1, § 8C2.6.

12. *Id.*

13. *Id.* § 8C2.7.

14. Since the decision in Arthur Andersen v. United States, 125 S.Ct. 2129 (2005), the prosecution must now prove that the person making the recommendation is aware that he or she is acting wrongfully in doing so. *See supra* chapter 5, notes 60–62 and accompanying text.

15. *See* United States v. Shotts, 145 F.3d 1289, 1300–01 (11th Cir. 1998) (concluding that a jury could find an obstruction of justice where the defendant advised an employee not to speak with federal investigators).

16. *See* United States v. Cioffi, 493 F.2d 1111 (2d Cir. 1974); Cole v. United States, 329 F.2d 437 (9th Cir. 1964); United States v. Cortese, 586 F. Supp. 119 (M.D. Pa. 1983). Once again, since the *Andersen* decision, the persuader would have to be aware of the wrongfulness of his or her action. For example, with regard to the assertion of one's Fifth Amendment rights, a persuader would be acting with consciousness of wrongdoing by recommending that a second party assert his or her Fifth Amendment rights in order to avoid incriminating not the second party, but the persuader. *See supra* chapter 5, note 61.

17. U.S.S.G., *supra* chapter 1, note 1, § 8B2.1(a)(1).

18. *Id.* § 8B2.1(b)(5)(A),(C).

19. *Id.* § 8B2.1(b)(6).

20. *Id.* § 8C2.5(g)(1).

21. *Id.*

22. *See* United States v. Rockwell Int'l Corp., 924 F.2d 928, 935 (9th Cir. 1991) (holding that a company's disclosure of fraud was untimely because the disclosure was made on the night before the indictment was announced).

23. U.S.S.G., *supra* chapter 1, note 1, § 8C2.5 cmt. 12.

24. *Id.*

25. *Id.* § 8C2.5 cmt. 13.

26. Rakoff et al., *supra* note 5, § 4.03[1].

27. *See* American College of Trial Lawyers, *The Erosion of the Attorney-Client Privilege and Work Product Doctrine in Federal Criminal Investigations*, 41 Duq. L. Rev. 307, 320 (2003); David M. Zornow & Keith D. Krakaur, *On the Brink of a Brave New World: The Death of Privilege in Corporate Criminal Investigations*, 37 Am. Crim. L. Rev. 147, 154–55 (2000).

28. *See* Memorandum from Deputy Attorney General Larry Thompson, U.S. Dep't of Justice, to Heads of Department Components, Principles of Federal Prosecution of Business Organizations (Jan. 20, 2003) [hereinafter Thompson Memorandum], *available at* http://www.usdoj.gov/dag/cftf/corporate_guidelines.htm. The Thompson Memorandum is a slightly revised version of the 1999 memorandum issued by Eric Holder to the same effect. *See* Memorandum from Deputy Attorney General Eric H. Holder, Jr., U.S. Dep't of Justice, to Heads of Department Components and All United States Attorneys, Federal Prosecution of Corporations (June 16, 1999) (summarizing factors prosecutors should take into account "in assessing the adequacy of a corporation's cooperation"), *available at* http://www.usdoj.gov/criminal/fraud/policy/Chargingcorps.html. The Thompson Memorandum states the Justice Department's policy regarding the decision to charge an organization with an offense, not its policy regarding the decision to recommend the cooperation reduction to an organization's culpability score. Thompson Memorandum, *supra*, § II(A). In practice, however, no distinction is made and the same policy is applied to both decisions. Indeed, with regard to the waiver of attorney-client privilege, the revisions to the Federal Sentencing Guidelines explicitly recognize the Department of Justice policy by stating that "[w]aiver of attorney-client privilege and of work product protections is not a prerequisite to a reduction in culpability score under subdivisions (1) and (2) of subsection (g) *unless such waiver is necessary in order to provide timely and thorough disclosure of all pertinent information known to the organization.*" U.S.S.G., *supra* chapter 1, note 1, § 8C2.5 cmt. 12 (emphasis added).

29. Thompson Memorandum, *supra* note 28, § VI(B); *see also* Zornow & Krakaur, *supra* note 27, at 154–56 (arguing that federal prosecutors' zealous application of the Federal Sentencing Guidelines have eviscerated the attorney-client privilege and the work-product doctrine).

30. Thompson Memorandum, *supra* note 28, § VI(B).

31. *See* Zornow & Krakaur, *supra* note 27, at 154 (stating that "[f]ederal prosecutors . . . now often insist, even at the outset of an investigation, that corporations turn over privileged communications, attorney work product, and incriminating statements from corporate employees as a condition of favorable treatment in the exercise of the prosecutor's considerable discretion."); *see also* Julie R. O'Sullivan, *Some Thoughts on Proposed Revisions to the Organizational Guidelines*, 1 Ohio St. J. Crim. L. 487, 495–96 (2004) ("Defense lawyers cite what they report to be regular governmental demands that corporations waive otherwise applicable privileges if they wish to avoid indictment or gain credit at sentencing for cooperating with the government as the principal impetus for the 'death' of corporate privileges. The defense bar clearly believes that federal prosecutors are, with increasing regularity, demanding that corporations waive the attorney-client privilege and work product protection as a condition of securing leniency in charging or at sentencing. According to defense practitioners,

'[w]aiver of the privilege is now a routine part of discussing a corporate resolution' of a criminal investigation.'').

Indeed, Professor O'Sullivan points out:

> The Arthur Andersen case may present a cautionary tale. Some argue that "[u]nder most objective standards, [Arthur Andersen, LLP] did everything in its power to avoid a prosecution that it knew would be a 'death penalty' for the firm,'' except agree to waive the attorney-client privilege. Thus, Andersen reportedly notified the Justice Department and SEC immediately upon learning of the document destruction in its Houston office. Andersen was also apparently willing to enter into a deferred prosecution agreement, "in essence a guilty plea, under which the government could have appointed a special monitor to oversee compliance with its new document retention policy and with other reforms to be approved by the DOJ.'' Finally, Andersen also agreed to expel the individuals responsible for the document destruction and did, of course, fire the head of Andersen's auditing team for Enron (and the government's cooperating witness in Andersen's criminal trial), David Duncan. Finally, Andersen "reportedly offered to pay as much as $750 million to Enron shareholders who had sued Andersen for its role in auditing Enron's books.'' Despite these efforts, the Department of Justice decided to seek an indictment and ultimately secured a conviction of the partnership.

Id. at 496 n.30 (citing Laurence A. Urgenson et al., *Attorney-Client Privilege: Surviving Corporate Fraud Scandal*, 9 Bus. Crimes Bull. 1, 6 (2002)).

32. Thompson Memorandum, *supra* note 28, § VI(B).

33. American College of Trial Lawyers, *supra* note 27, at 319.

34. Zornow & Krakaur, *supra* note 27, at 179.

35. *Id.* at 154; *see also* E. Lawrence Barcella, Jr. et al., *Cooperation with Government Is a Growing Trend*, Nat'l L.J., July 19, 2004, at S2 (suggesting that the increase in investigation and prosecution of corporate crime evinces a trend in which cooperation "with the government—not by choice—is often the only road to survival for both corporations and their executives.'').

36. Thompson Memorandum, *supra* note 28, § VI(B).

37. Interestingly, because the laws of several states require organizations to pay the legal fees of employees under investigation, the Thompson Memorandum includes a footnote indicating that payment of legal fees in such cases cannot be regarded as a failure to cooperate. *See id.* § 4 n.4.

38. Barcella Jr. et al., *supra* note 35, at S2 (emphasis added).

39. *Id.*

40. *Id.*

41. Michele Galen, *Keeping the Long Arm of the Law at Arm's Length*, Bus. Wk., Apr. 22, 1991, at 104.

42. Barcella Jr. et al., *supra* note 35, at S2.

43. Israel & LaFave, *supra* chapter 3, note 17, at 26.

44. *See supra* chapter 3, note 19 and accompanying text.

45. *See* Winthrop Swenson, *The Organizational Guidelines' "Carrot and Stick" Philosophy, and Their Focus on "Effective" Compliance, in* White Collar Crime: Law and Practice 782, 785 (Jerold H. Israel et al. eds., 1st ed. 1996) (articulating that the guidelines' third objective is "to create incentives for companies to take crime controlling actions.'').

46. *See supra* text accompanying chapter 4, notes 24–26.

47. This policy, which was implicit before November 1, 2004, is now explicitly recognized by the Guidelines. *See* U.S.S.G., *supra* chapter 1, note 1, § 8C2.5 cmt. 12 (providing that "[w]aiver of attorney-client privilege and of work product protections is not a prerequisite to a reduction in culpability score . . . *unless such waiver is necessary in order to provide timely and thorough disclosure of all pertinent information* known to the organization.") (emphasis added); *see also* Zornow & Krakaur, *supra* note 27, at 155–56 (contending that the ambiguous word "necessary" used in the Thompson Memorandum, and now enshrined in the Organizational Sentencing Guidelines, enables federal prosecutors to obtain a corporation's waiver of attorney-client privilege).

48. *See* Upjohn Co. v. United States, 449 U.S. 383, 395 (1981).

49. *Id.*

50. *Id.* at 396 (quoting Philadelphia v. Westinghouse Elec. Corp., 205 F. Supp. 830, 831 (E.D. Pa. 1962)).

51. *See* Laurie P. Cohen, *Prosecutor's Tough New Tactics Turn Firms Against Employees*, Wall St. J., June 4, 2004, at A1.

52. Thompson Memorandum, *supra* note 28, VI.B.

Chapter 7

1. *See* Milton Friedman, Capitalism and Freedom 133 (1962); *see also* John Hasnas, *The Normative Theories of Business Ethics: A Guide for the Perplexed*, 8 Bus. Ethics Q. 19, 21–25 (1998).

2. William M. Evan & R. Edward Freeman, *A Stakeholder Theory of the Modern Corporation: Kantian Capitalism, in* Ethical Theory and Business 75 (Tom L. Beauchamp & Norman E. Bowie eds., 4th ed., 1993); *see also* Hasnas, *supra* note 1, at 25–28.

3. *See* Thomas Donaldson & Thomas W. Dunfee, *Toward a Unified Conception of Business Ethics: Integrative Social Contracts Theory*, 19 Acad. Mgmt. Rev. 252 (1994); *see also* Hasnas, *supra* note 1, at 29–30.

4. In other words, becoming a businessperson may subject individuals to the additional ethical obligations specified by the various theories of business ethics, but it does not relieve them of any of the obligations they possess as human beings. Becoming the agent of an organization's owners or stakeholders, or of society at large, does not empower one to take actions that would be unethical if they were undertaken on one's own behalf. Dennis P. Quinn & Thomas M. Jones, *An Agent Morality View of Business Policy*, 20 Acad. Mgmt. Rev. 22, 37–38 (1995).

Chapter 8

1. Aristotle, The Nicomachean Ethics bk. 5 (D.A. Rees ed., Oxford Univ. Press 1951).

2. *See* Norman Bowie, Business Ethics 141 (1982); Sissela Bok, *Whistleblowing and Professional Responsibilities, in* Ethical Theory and Business 306 (Tom L. Beauchamp & Norman E. Bowie eds., 4th ed. 1993).

3. *See* Patricia H. Werhane, *Employee and Employer Rights in an Institutional Context, in* Ethical Theory and Business 270–71 (Tom L. Beauchamp & Norman E. Bowie eds., 3d ed. 1988) (explaining that in exchange for working for, being fair to, and respecting their employers, employees should expect fair pay, privacy, and due process in the workplace).

4. *See supra* text accompanying chapter 6, notes 20–43.

5. *See* U.S.S.G., *supra* chapter 1, note 1, § 8C2.5(g)(1) (noting that, for a corporation to meet its timeliness requirement, it must report or take action against an employee before a government investigation begins); *supra* text accompanying chapter 6, notes 21–22 (same).

6. *See supra* text accompanying chapter 5, notes 68–79.

7. *See, e.g.,* Jason A. Colquitt et al., *Justice at the Millennium: A Meta-Analytical Review of 25 Years of Organizational Justice Research*, 86 J. Applied Psychol. 425, 426 (2000).

8. Organizational justice researchers define procedural justice in terms of six criteria:

[T]o be perceived as fair, [p]rocedures should (a) be applied consistently across people and across time, (b) be free from bias (e.g., ensuring that a third party has no vested interest in a particular settlement), (c) ensure that accurate information is collected and used in making decisions, (d) have some mechanism to correct flawed or inaccurate decisions, (e) conform to personal or prevailing standards of ethics or morality, and (f) ensure that the opinions of various groups affected by the decision have been taken into account.

Id. at 426.

9. *Id.* at 434.

10. *See* Marshall Sashkin & Richard L. Williams, *Does Fairness Make a Difference?*, 19 Organizational Dynamics 56, 57 (1990).

11. *See* Evan & Freeman, *supra* chapter 7, note 2, at 97 (noting that under the stakeholder theory, managers owe a fiduciary duty to all stakeholders, including suppliers, customers, employees, and community members); *see also* Thomas Donaldson, Corporations and Morality 57 (1982) (revealing that social contract theorists believe that organizations' underlying functions are to promote social welfare to consumers and employees).

12. *See* Hasnas, *supra* chapter 7, note 1, at 22 (stating that the stockholder theory poses the view that managers have the sole duty of increasing profits by any legal, nonfraudulent means possible).

Chapter 9

1. *See* George Orwell, 1984 (1949).

2. Rogene Buchholz, *Privacy, in* The Blackwell Encyclopedic Dictionary of Business Ethics 504 (Patricia H. Werhane & R. Edward Freeman eds., 1997).

3. Laura B. Pincus & Clayton Trotter, *The Disparity between Public and Private Sector Employee Privacy Protections: A Call for Legitimate Privacy Rights for Private Sector Workers*, 33 Am. Bus. L.J. 51, 54 (2001).

4. For example,

Drug and alcohol testing through hair follicles reveals data relating to the subject's personal life for a period of up to six months for a three-inch section of hair. Employee monitoring or surveillance systems infiltrate the worker's daily environment, yielding information as banal as how many times the individual takes bathroom breaks during the work day. In one instance, telephone calls received by airline reservation agents were electronically monitored on a second-by-second basis; agents were allowed only eleven seconds between each call and twelve minutes of break time each day. In fact, it is estimated that American employers monitor more than 750 calls every minute.

Surveillance permeates other areas of the work place, as well. Employers monitor the key-strokes of two-thirds of all computer operators, and complaints of employer e-mail intrusions are increasing. A recent *MacWorld* survey found that twenty-two percent of large businesses in a variety of industries "engaged in searches of employee computer files, voice mail, electronic mail, or other networking communications," and fewer than one-third of these companies warn the workers that such surveillance is taking place.

Id. at 52–53.

5. *See* Evan & Freeman, *supra* chapter 7, note 2, at 101.

6. *See* Laura P. Hartman, *Technology and Ethics: Privacy in the Workplace*, 106 Bus. & Soc'y Rev. 1, 17 (2001). In contemporary social contract terminology, the right to privacy constitutes a "hypernorm"—a principle "so fundamental to human existence that [it] serve[s] as a guide in evaluating lower level moral norms," Donaldson & Dunfee, *supra* chapter 7, note 3, at 265—that all business organizations are required to respect.

7. *See* BOWIE, *supra* chapter 8, note 2, at 90–91; *see also* Pincus & Trotter, *supra* note 3, at 56.

8. Pincus & Trotter, *supra* note 3, at 88.

9. *See* George Brenkert, *Privacy, Polygraphs, and Work, in* BUSINESS ETHICS: READINGS AND CASES IN CORPORATE MORALITY 294, 295 (W. Michael Hoffman & Jennifer Mills Moore eds., 2d ed. 1990) (noting that "the information to which the employer . . . is entitled . . . is that information which regards his possible acceptable performance of the services for which he might be hired."); *see also* Joseph R. Des Jardins & Ronald Duska, *Drug Testing in Employment, in* BUSINESS ETHICS: READINGS AND CASES IN CORPORATE MORALITY 301, 302 (W. Michael Hoffman & Jennifer Mills Moore eds., 2d ed. 1990) (explaining that "an employee's right to privacy is violated whenever personal information is . . . collected, and/or used by an employer in a way or for any purpose that is irrelevant to . . . [their] contractual relationship.").

10. U.S.S.G., *supra* chapter 1, note 1, § 8B2.1(b).

11. *Id.* § 8B2.1(b)(3) (emphasis added).

12. *Id.* § 8B2.1(b)(5)(A) (emphasis added).

Chapter 10

1. *See* Evan & Freeman, *supra* chapter 7, note 2, at 97; *see also* Hasnas, *supra* chapter 7, note 1, at 27.

2. *See* DONALDSON, *supra* chapter 8, note 11, at 53; *see also* Hasnas, *supra* chapter 7, note 1, at 30–31.

3. *See* FRIEDMAN, *supra* chapter 7, note 1, at 133 (stating that "there is one and only one social responsibility of business—to use its resources and engage in activities designed to increase its profits so long as it stays within the rules of the game, which is to say, engages in open and free competition without deception or fraud.").

4. *See* James A. Waters, *Catch 20.5: Corporate Morality as an Organizational Phenomenon, in* CONTEMPORARY MORAL CONTROVERSIES IN BUSINESS 160 (A. Pablo Iannone ed., 1989); *see also* DONALDSON, *supra* chapter 8, note 11, at 154–55 (describing how many U.S. companies utilize "hot-lines" and "operator" policies to encourage employees to speak truthfully).

5. Upjohn Co. v. United States, 449 U.S. 383, 383 (1981).

6. *Id.* at 391.

7. *Id.* at 392.

8. *Id.* (citation omitted).

9. *See supra* chapter 6, notes 20–43, chapter 8, note 4 and accompanying text.

10. U.S.S.G., *supra* chapter 1, note 1, § 8C2.5 cmt. 12.

11. *See supra* chapter 6, notes 28–35 and accompanying text.

12. U.S.S.G., *supra* chapter 1, note 1, § 8C2.5(g)(1).

13. Upjohn Co., 449 U.S. at 393.

14. U.S.S.G., *supra* chapter 1, note 1, § 8B2.1(b)(5)(C).

15. *See* Practising Law Institute, *Report of the Ad Hoc Advisory Group on the Organizational Sentencing Guidelines*, 1417 PLI/CORP 159, 243–47 (2004). In its report, the Ad Hoc Advisory Group on the Organizational Sentencing Guidelines recommended amending the guidelines to make the requirement of anonymity, if not confidentiality, explicit by requiring organizations "to have a system whereby the organization's employees and agents may report or seek guidance regarding potential or actual violations of law without fear of retaliation, *including mechanisms to allow for anonymous reporting.*" Id. at 249 (emphasis added). The Sentencing Commission proposed that the amendments to the guidelines weaken this requirement somewhat, requiring organizations "to have and publicize a system, *which may include mechanisms that allow for anonymity or confidentiality,* whereby the organization's employees and agents may report or seek guidance regarding potential or actual criminal conduct without fear of retaliation." Notice of Submission to Congress of Amendments to The Sentencing Guidelines Effective November 1, 2004, 69 Fed. Reg. 28994, 29019 (proposed May 19, 2004).

16. Sarbanes-Oxley Act of 2002, Pub. L. No. 107-204, § 301, 116 Stat. 745, 776 (emphasis added).

17. *Id.* § 8C2.5 cmt. 12.

Chapter 11

1. Edward Soule, *Trust and Managerial Responsibility*, 8 BUS. ETHICS Q. 249, 268 (1998).

2. *See* LaRue Tone Hosmer, *Why Be Moral? A Different Rationale for Managers*, 4 BUS. ETHICS Q. 191, 202 (1994) (stating that "managers can build trust over time only by treating the members of the stakeholder groups in ways that they consider to be 'right' and 'just' and 'fair.'").

3. *Id.* at 192 ("We can ... legitimately make the claim that acting in ways that can be considered to be 'right' and 'just' and 'fair' *is absolutely essential to the long-term competitive success of the firm.*"); *see also* FRANK K. SONNENBERG, MANAGING WITH A CONSCIENCE: HOW TO IMPROVE PERFORMANCE THROUGH INTEGRITY, TRUST, AND COMMITMENT 188 (1996) (arguing that without trust, no company can ever hope for excellence). *See also* Bryan W. Husted, *The Ethical Limits of Trust in Business Relations*, 8 BUS. ETHICS Q. 233, 233 (1998).

4. Hosmer, *supra* note 2, at 193.

5. Thomas M. Jones, *Instrumental Stakeholder Theory: A Synthesis of Ethics and Economics*, 20 ACAD. MGMT. REV. 404, 422 (1995) (emphasis added).

6. *Id.; see also* RICHARD A. EPSTEIN, FORBIDDEN GROUNDS 60–72 (1992) (asserting that employers and employees are linked together in a common venture and arguing that an organization can reduce costs associated with resolving internal conflicts and dissatisfaction by developing rules that satisfy all of its members).

7. George G. Brenkert, *Trust, Morality and International Business*, 8 Bus. Ethics Q. 293, 305 (1998); *see* LaRue Tone Hosmer, *Trust: The Connecting Link Between Organizational Theory and Philosophical Ethics*, 20 Acad. Mgmt. Rev. 379, 390 (1995):

> Trust generally occurs under conditions of vulnerability to the interests of the individual and dependence upon the behavior of other people. An essential part of the definition of trust is the expectation that the loss if trust is broken will be much greater than the gain when trust is maintained; otherwise, the decision to trust would be simple economic rationality.

8. Hosmer, *supra* note 7, at 392.

9. Brenkert, *supra* note 7, at 307.

10. *Id.*

11. Hosmer, *supra* note 7, at 393.

12. Hosmer, *supra* note 7, at 392.

13. For evidence that this is not merely idle speculation, see Stanley S. Arkin & Charles Sullivan, *Business Crime: Attacking Corporate Attorney-Client Privilege and Work Product*, N.Y.L.J., May 4, 2004, at 3 (reporting on the effect organizations' cooperation with the government can have on their employees' attitudes), Barcella, *supra* chapter 6, note 35, at 52 col. 1, and Cohen, *supra* chapter 6, note 51.

14. Brenkert, *supra* note 7, at 307.

15. *See generally* James A. Waters, *Catch 20.5: Corporate Morality as an Organizational Phenomenon, in* Contemporary Moral Controversies in Business 160 (A. Pablo Iannone ed., 1989) (arguing that a system of "secret informers" will destroy the spirit of openness that an organization seeks).

16. *Id.*

17. *E.g.*, Jonathan D. Glater, *Enron Holders in Pact With Andersen Overseas Firms*, N.Y. Times, Aug. 28, 2002, at C3 (illustrating the effects of an indictment on a financial services company).

Chapter 12

1. Waters, *supra* chapter 11, note 15, at 153.

2. *Id.*

3. *Id.* at 153–57.

4. *See* Robert Jackall, *Moral Mazes: Bureaucracy and Managerial Work*, 5 Harv. Bus. Rev., Sept.–Oct. 1983, at 120 (claiming that a prominent characteristic of the authority system in American businesses is that details are pushed down and credit is pushed up, thus creating great pressure on middle managers not only to transmit good news but also to protect their corporations, their bosses, and themselves in the process).

5. United States v. Bank of New England, 821 F.2d 844, 856 (1st Cir. 1987).

6. *See supra* text accompanying chapter 4, notes 15–21.

7. *See supra* text accompanying chapter 10, note 4.

8. The Thompson Memorandum allows federal prosecutors to consider an organization's cooperation in deciding whether to bring an indictment against it, but it clearly does not require them to refrain from indicting cooperating organizations. *See* Thompson Memorandum, *supra* chapter 6, note 28, § VI(B) (stating, "[A] corporation's offer of cooperation does not automatically entitle it to immunity from prosecution. A corporation should not be able to escape liability merely by offering up its directors, officers, employees, or agents as in lieu of its own prosecution."). In its testimony before the Ad Hoc Advisory Group on the Organizational Sentencing

Guidelines, the Department of Justice made clear that it considers a reduction in penalty, not immunity from prosecution, to be the proper reward for an organization's cooperation, stating that "[w]e also believe the guidelines appropriately encourage and reward full and meaningful cooperation by permitting a corporation to reduce its punishment by lowering its culpability score if the corporation thoroughly discloses all pertinent information—specifically information that is sufficient for the government to identify the nature and extent of the offense and the individuals responsible for the criminal conduct." Testimony of the U.S. Department of Justice 10 (Nov. 14, 2002), *available at* http://www.ussc.gov/corp/ph11_02/t_comey.pdf.

Furthermore, it is clear that organizations possess no self-evaluation privilege that entitles them to withhold the results of their self-assessments from federal prosecutors or any government agency. *See* Fed. Trade Comm'n v. TRW, Inc., 628 F.2d 207, 210 (D.C. Cir. 1980) (holding that "[w]hatever may be the status of the 'self-evaluative' privilege in the context of private litigation, courts with apparent uniformity have refused its application, where . . . the documents in question have been sought by a governmental agency"); *see also* Catherine L. Fornias, *The Fifth Circuit Reconsiders Application of the Work Product Doctrine and Privilege of Self-Evaluation: In Re* Kaiser Aluminum & Chemical Co., 76 Tul. L. Rev. 247, 252 (2001).

9. U.S.S.G., *supra* chapter 1, note 1, § 8C2.5 cmt. 12.

10. *See* United States v. Mass. Inst. of Tech., 129 F.3d 681, 685 (1st Cir. 1997) (describing selective waiver as "the provision of otherwise privileged communications to one outsider while withholding them from another.").

11. David A. Nadler, *Don't Ask, Don't Tell*, Wall St. J., Nov. 25, 2003, at B2.

12. *Id.*

Chapter 13

1. U.S.S.G., *supra* chapter 1, note 1, § 8C2.5(g)(1).

2. *Id.* § 8C2.5 cmt. 12.

3. Thompson Memorandum, *supra* chapter 6, note 28, § VI(B).

4. U.S.S.G., *supra* chapter 1, note 1, § 8B2.1 cmt. 5.

5. *Id.* § 8C2.5 cmt. 13.

6. Because Lie is no longer an Endrun employee, the prosecution cannot get access to documents in his possession by the usual stratagem of issuing a subpoena to Lie in his corporate capacity. *See* United States v. John Doe #1, John Doe #2, John Doe #3 (*In re* Three Grand Jury Subpoenas Duces Tecum Dated Jan. 29, 1999), 191 F.3d 173, 183 (2d Cir. 1999) (concluding that ex-employees may refuse to provide documents of a corporation where they previously worked by claiming a Fifth Amendment right of production privilege). Thus, unless the prosecution can meet the "foregone conclusion" test, it cannot constitutionally get access to the documents in Lie's possession without the corporation's help. *See* United States v. Hubbell, 530 U.S. 27, 44–45 (2000) (holding that documents were not a foregone conclusion where the government failed to show it had prior knowledge of the existence and whereabouts of such documents); Fisher v. United States, 425 U.S. 391, 411 (1976) (holding that admitting to the existence and location of papers is a foregone conclusion and does not amount to the level of testimony protected by the Fifth Amendment).

7. Consider, for example, the law of statutory rape, and various aspects of the law of conspiracy, and of felony murder.

8. New York Central & Hudson River Railroad Co. v. United States, 212 U.S. 481, 494–95 (1909).

9. *Id.* at 495–96. The courts were still adhering to this justification three-quarters of a century later, holding, for example, that organizations were strictly liable for the actions of their employees on the ground that the "identification of the particular agents responsible for a Sherman Act violation is especially difficult, and their conviction and punishment is peculiarly ineffective as a deterrent. At the same time, conviction and punishment of the business entity itself is likely to be both appropriate and effective." United States v. Hilton Hotels Corp., 467 F.2d 1000, 1006 (9th Cir. 1972).

10. Morissette v. United States, 342 U.S. 246, 254 (1952).

11. *Id.* at 256.

12. United States v. Maze, 414 U.S. 395, 407 (1974) (Burger, C.J., dissenting).

13. Organized Crime Control Act of 1970, Pub. L. No. 91-452, § 1, 84 Stat. 922, 993 (1970).

14. Braswell v. United States, 487 U.S. 99, 115 (1988).

15. Williams, Jr. & Whitney, *supra* chapter 5, note 78, at 15.

16. Glater, *supra* chapter 11, note 17, at C3.

Index

About the Author

John Hasnas is an associate professor at the McDonough School of Business at Georgetown University in Washington, DC, where he teaches courses in ethics and law. He has held a previous appointment as an associate professor of law at George Mason University, where he taught courses in criminal law and white-collar crime. He has been a visiting scholar at the Kennedy Institute of Ethics in Washington, DC, and at the Social Philosophy and Policy Center in Bowling Green, Ohio. Between 1997 and 1999, he served as assistant general counsel to Koch Industries, Inc., in Wichita, Kansas. He holds a J.D. and a Ph.D. in legal philosophy from Duke University. He lives in Falls Church, Virginia.